A HISTORY OF
MULTICULTURAL AMERICA

World War II to the New Frontier
1940-1963

William Loren Katz

RSVP
**RAINTREE
STECK-VAUGHN**
P U B L I S H E R S
The Steck-Vaughn Company

Austin, Texas

For Laurie

Cover and interior design: Joyce Spicer
Electronic Production: Scott Melcer

Library of Congress Cataloging-in-Publication Data

Katz, William Loren.
    World War II to the new frontier, 1940-1963 / by William Loren Katz.
        p.   cm. — (A history of multicultural America)
    Includes bibliographical references and index.
    Summary: A multicultural history of the United States, from World War II through the 1960's March on Washington, discussing the experiences of minorities and women during this period.
        ISBN 0-8114-6280-3   —   ISBN 0-8114-2917-2 (soft cover)
    1. Pluralism (Social sciences) — United States — Juvenile literature.
2. Minorities — United States — Juvenile literature.   3. United States —
Race relations — Juvenile literature.   [1. United States — History —
20th century.   2. Minorities — History.   3. Afro-Americans — History
— 1877-1964.]   I. Title.   II. Series: Katz, William Loren. History of
multicultural America.
E184.A1K2975   1993
305.8'00973—dc20   92-42801
                                                                           CIP
                                                                            AC

Printed and bound in the United States of America

1 2 3 4 5 6 7 8 9 0 LB 98 97 96 95 94 93

Acknowledgments

All prints from the collection of the author, William L. Katz, with the following exceptions: pp. 17t, 24, 26, 48 (both), 51t, 52, 53b, 56, 57, 65, 69, 76, 79b, 80 (both) AP/Wide World; pp. 11, 16, 21t, 23t, 36, 39b, 41, 44, 51b, 53t, 59, 64, 73b, 75, 79t, 84, 87, 89b, 90, 91, 93 (both) UPI/Bettmann; p. 39c Pach/Bettmann; pp. 17b, 18, 73t U.S. Army; pp. 7, 10, 21t, 23b, 27 (both), 31 Library of Congress; pp. 32, 33, 60, 62, 63b, 67, 89t © Life Magazine; pp. 12t, 14 National Archives; p. 19t © William A. Scott, 761st Battalion; p. 21b © Gordan Parks; p. 47 United Nations, Office of Public Information; p. 58 © Focus on Sports, p. 61 NAACP; p. 81 © Gene Daniels/Black Star.

Cover photographs: (inset) UPI/Bettmann; (map) Department of the Army, Center of Military History.

TABLE OF CONTENTS

INTRODUCTION

The history of the United States is the story of people of many backgrounds. A few became wealthy through their knowledge of science, industry, or banking. But it was ordinary people who most shaped the progress of this country and created our national heritage.

The American experience, however, has often been recounted in history books as the saga of powerful men—presidents and senators, merchants and industrialists. Schoolchildren were taught that the wisdom and patriotism of an elite created democracy and prosperity.

A truthful history of the United States has to do more than celebrate the contributions of the few. Ordinary Americans fought the Revolution that set this country free, and ordinary workers built the nation's economy. The overwhelming majority of people held no office, made little money, and worked hard all their lives.

Some groups, women and minorities in particular, had to vault legal barriers and public hostility in order to make their contributions to the American dream, only to find that school courses taught little about their achievements. The valiant struggle of minorities and women to win dignity, equality, and justice often was omitted from history's account. Some believe this omission was accidental or careless, others insist it was purposeful.

Native Americans struggled valiantly to survive military and cultural assaults on their lives. But the public was told Native Americans were savages undeserving of any rights to their land or culture. African Americans battled to break the chains of slavery and to scale the walls of racial discrimination. But a century after slavery ended, some textbooks still pictured African Americans as content under slavery and bewildered by freedom. Arrivals from Asia, Mexico, and the West Indies faced legal restrictions and sometimes violence. But the public was told that they were undeserving of a welcome because they took "American jobs," and some were "treacherous aliens."

Whether single, married, or mothers, women were portrayed as dependent on men and accepting of a lowly status. The record of their sturdy labors, enduring strengths, and their arduous struggle to achieve equality rarely found its way into classrooms. The version of American history that reached the public carried many prejudices. It often preferred farmers over urban workers, middle classes over working classes, rich over poor. Women and minorities became invisible, ineffective, or voiceless.

This distorted legacy also failed to mention the campaigns waged by minorities and women to attain human rights. Such efforts did not reflect glory on white male rulers and their unwillingness to extend democracy and opportunity to others.

This kind of history was not a trustworthy tale. It locked out entire races and impeded racial understanding. Not only was it unreliable, but for most students it was dull and boring.

Our history has to be truthful and complete. Our struggle to overcome the barriers of nature and obstacles made by humans is an inspiring story. This series of books seeks to explore the heroic efforts of minorities and women to find their place in the American dream.

William Loren Katz

CHAPTER 1

TOWARD WORLD WAR

Fascist dictatorships had gained power in Italy under Benito Mussolini in 1922 and in Germany under Adolf Hitler in 1933. In 1936 Hitler and Mussolini signed a military alliance with the military dictatorship in Japan to form the Axis Powers. By 1939, much of the world was at war against Fascist imperialism.

Italian Americans, German Americans, and Japanese Americans showed little sympathy for their original homelands. A steady flow of refugees — Czechs, Poles, Jews, Catholics, liberals, and others — fled Fascist-occupied Europe. Through their terrifying stories, ethnic communities learned of Fascism's danger to the world. Some sounded alarms about the threat to the United States.

However, the United States remained neutral. Some American corporate executives encouraged Hitler and Mussolini through trade and loans. They liked Fascism's strong anticommunist talk and cared little if Fascists persecuted innocent minorities.

American immigration laws of the day had rigid quotas designed to restrict immigration. It was the time of the Great Depression, and millions were jobless. Congress and union leaders warned that refugees would "take American jobs." President Franklin D. Roosevelt (FDR), asked about admitting Jewish refugees, said it was not being considered since "We have the quota system."

In 1939 Congress debated a bill to admit 20,000 Jewish children under age 14 who faced concentration camps in Europe. Thousands of American families agreed to adopt the children, and the Quakers agreed to pay for and make all arrangements. But Secretary of State Cordell Hull said the bill meant hiring more officials and using "additional office space," and Congress said it would increase unemployment. The bill was defeated. The fate of the children was sealed when Nazi armies occupied Europe.

In May 1939, 930 German Jews, carrying passports the Nazis

had stamped with a red "J," left on the steamship *St. Louis* for the Americas. Some held legal U.S. immigration numbers. While the *St. Louis* and its human cargo, including 400 women and children, drifted off the coast of Miami, Florida, American Jewish leaders urged FDR, the State Department, and the Congress to admit the refugees. It was no use, and the *St. Louis* had to return to Europe. Until they were overrun by Nazi armies the next year, Holland and France were able to offer the refugees safety.

In the 1930s a quarter of a million refugees, mostly European Jews, did enter the United States. These refugees included prominent scholars, writers, scientists, and theologians. Thomas Mann, who had received the Nobel Prize for Literature in 1929, decided to remain here after his criticism of Nazism made it dangerous for him to return.

Paul Tillich, a famous theologian, philosopher, and college professor, fled Hitler's Germany for Harvard University. "I have the great honor and luck," he said, "to be the first non-Jewish professor dismissed from a German university." Tillich's three-volume *Systematic Theology* is considered one of the greatest religious works of the 20th century.

Albert Einstein, a German Jew who received the Nobel Prize in 1921 for his work in theoretical physics, was visiting California when Hitler gained power. When he heard that his property was seized and his German citizenship cancelled, he settled in the United States and taught at Princeton University. A patriotic society opposed admitting Einstein, calling him a "Communist" and saying his theory of relativity had "no scientific value."

Albert Einstein (center) shown with fellow scientist and German immigrant Charles Steinmetz in the early 1920s.

Some Americans ran an antifascist rescue mission. Alvin S. Johnson, born to Danish immigrants living in Nebraska in 1874, had become head of the New School for Social Research in New York City in the 1920s. Johnson was shocked by the Nazi firing of distinguished anti-Nazi, Jewish, and Catholic college professors.

"I want to make what return I can for liberties I have enjoyed," Johnson concluded. He planned to hire these outstanding academics for an American "University in Exile." In 1940 some recruiters from

New York University and Princeton's Institute for Advanced Studies joined his daring plan.

Johnson and the others sent agents to rescue professors fleeing Hitler's march through Europe. American Jewish societies took a leading role in the effort as well as Catholic, Quaker, Unitarian, and a number of nonsectarian relief organizations.

Professor Varian Fry flew to Marseilles, France, on a month's vacation to direct a rescue operation under the noses of the pro-Nazi Vichy government. Prominent refugees were hiding there or were being held in Vichy jails. Fry stayed 13 months and became an expert at having passports forged, tracing people in hiding, and bribing Vichy officials to release prisoners. He and his associates were trailed, spied upon, and raided by the Vichy police. Fry was finally expelled. But he had aided 1,500 important escapees to find safety. His successor aided 300.

Hans Sahl, a writer, described meeting Fry when he felt most helpless.

> ...life is as good as over — and suddenly a young American in shirtsleeves is stuffing your pockets full of money, putting his arm around your shoulders, and whispering with the conspiratorial expression of a ham actor: "Oh there are ways to get you out of here," [and he]... takes a silk handkerchief from his jacket and says: "Here, have this. Sorry it isn't cleaner." You know, since that day I have loved America.

Enrico Fermi

Once here, more than three-fourths of the writers, scholars, dentists, doctors, architects, psychologists, chemists, professors, musicians, artists, and clergymen resumed their professions. Many made extraordinary contributions to their new homeland.

Part of the antifascist refugee flow included physicists of world renown. They were delighted to be free and ready to employ their knowledge and America's fine experimental machinery against Hitler and Mussolini.

Enrico Fermi, who had won the Nobel Prize in Physics in 1938, left Italy the next year and became a professor at Columbia University. That year Danish physicist Niels Bohr arrived carrying important data from Lise Meitner, a German Jewish scientist who fled Germany to Sweden. Meitner had heard that German scientific teams had worked with uranium and neutrons and had produced barium. Bohr rushed to Fermi who decided that Germany would be able to build a chain-reaction nuclear bomb.

Fermi contacted scientist Leo Szilard, a Hungarian refugee, who also became alarmed. With Eugene Wigner, another Hungarian refugee, Szilard drove out to see Albert Einstein on Long Island. Einstein immediately agreed, the President of the United States had to be told. With Edward Teller, another Hungarian refugee, Einstein drafted a letter to Roosevelt that described the theory of nuclear energy and its potential in bombs.

The government moved slowly on a nuclear energy project until Pearl Harbor, but then it wanted a nuclear bomb. Robert Oppenheimer, a Jewish American, was placed in charge of the team of refugee scientists at the "Manhattan Project" seeking to develop the first nuclear weapon.

Success largely rested on people who had escaped Hitler. Stanislaus Ulam, a Polish-born mathematician who arrived in the United States in 1935, was an important contributor. So was Professor George Kistiakovsky, a Ukrainian American who became a consultant in 1943 to the Los Alamos Project and later director of the explosives division of the Manhattan Project. Working at the Los Alamos plant in 1945, Armenian American Harry Daghlian lost his life while conducting experiments with the plutonium to be fitted into the first atomic bomb.

The rise of Fascism had another impact on America. More than Roosevelt's New Deal, it lifted the United States out of the Great Depression by creating huge demands for American goods. By 1940, as factory orders poured in, plants closed during the depression began to reopen, and workers were rehired.

The defense industry boomed but rarely hired people of color. For example, in New York City only 142 out of 300,000 defense jobs were held by African Americans. Black people were also asked to accept being drafted into a totally segregated army.

In September 1940, Walter White and A. Philip Randolph submitted a plan to the President to insure equality for African American soldiers. The administration made promises. Blacks would be trained as officers, for example, but in separate camps.

Civil rights crusader A. Philip Randolph

A crusader for racial justice and the leading black union leader in America, Randolph called for a massive protest march on Washington on July 1. "The administration," he was convinced, "will never give the Negro justice until they see masses — ten, twenty, fifty thousand Negroes on the White House lawn."

Randolph meant business and had widespread support. FDR sent New York City mayor La Guardia and Eleanor Roosevelt to negotiate with Randolph. When he did not budge, FDR invited Randolph to the White House. Facing the President, the secretary of war, and the secretary of the navy, Randolph demanded action.

Finally, as the day of the march neared, the President agreed to compromise. On June 25, 1941, FDR's Executive Order No. 8802 ended hiring on the basis of "race, creed, color, or national origin" in the defense plants. It opened jobs for African Americans, Filipino Americans, and other people of color.

The order also established the first federal Fair Employment Practices Commission (FEPC) to investigate any violations. To people of color, FDR had issued the most significant federal document since Lincoln's Emancipation Proclamation.

The order came just in time. Six months later, the United States was at war and would need every ounce of its strength and unity to defeat the most powerful force on earth.

Wendell Willkie Broadcasts to Germany

In November 1940, Wendell Willkie was the Republican presidential candidate FDR defeated. In February 1941, Willkie broadcast to Germany:

> I am purely of German descent. My family name is not Willkie, but Willicke. My grandparents left Germany 90 years ago because... they demanded the right to live as free men. I, too, claim that right.

> I am proud of my German blood. But I hate aggression and tyranny. And my convictions are shared by the overwhelming majority of my fellow countrymen of German descent. They too, believe in freedom and human rights.... We German Americans reject and hate the aggression and lust for power of the present German government. ∎

"The Sacred Rights of the Jewish People"

In October 1938, the only African American in Congress, Arthur Mitchell of Illinois, asked President Roosevelt to save the Jews of Germany.

> We believe that the same spirit of intolerance which is working so tremendously against the safety and sacred rights of the Jewish people, if permitted to go unchallenged, will manifest itself sooner or later against all minority groups, perhaps in all parts of the world. We request you [President Roosevelt], the highest representative of our Government, to use every reasonable and peaceable means at your command in securing protection for the Jewish people in this hour of sad calamity.

The Roosevelt administration did not heed Mitchell's words of advice. A month later Germany escalated its anti-Semitic campaign with its *Kristallnacht* or "night of broken glass." Nazi crowds stormed into Jewish neighborhoods to destroy stores and homes.

Hitler's "final solution" — genocide of the world's Jews — was being enacted. The calamity Mitchell had warned about was about to engulf Jews, Eastern Europeans, Catholics, Russians, Gypsies, homosexuals, Communists, and anyone who dared to oppose Nazism. ∎

Congressman Arthur Mitchell and his wife

CHAPTER 2

WORLD WAR II

Dorie Miller

*Colin Kelly,
air ace*

From the day of the attack on Pearl Harbor, December 7, 1941, America's ethnic groups and women proved crucial to the country's war effort. Black sailor Dorie Miller, boxing champion of the battleship *West Virginia*, was a messmate (waiter or busboy) without combat training. But as Japanese planes bombed the *West Virginia*, Miller dropped the laundry he had been carrying and sprang into action. First he rescued his captain from the burning deck. Then he helped man the ship's antiaircraft guns.

Miller claimed that he brought down six Japanese Zeros. The Navy gave him credit for four. In May 1942, Admiral Chester Nimitz pinned the Navy Cross on Miller. In 1944 Miller was still a messmate when he went down with his new ship, the *Liscomb Bay*. Most African Americans remained messmates throughout the war.

The first U.S. Army Air Corps victory came three days after Pearl Harbor. Captain Colin Kelly, 26, an Irish American and a graduate of West Point, and Sgt. Meyer Levin, his Jewish American bombardier, sank the Japanese battleship *Haruna* in the Pacific.

The first American ethnic community to demonstrate its support of the war were Japanese Americans living in Hawaii. During the December 7 raid, 2,000 Japanese American soldiers defended the base at Pearl Harbor and were assisted by Japanese American civilians. Some gave blood at Queens Hospital, and others drove trucks for Oahu's Citizens' Defense Committee. Said one:

> Most of us have lived longer in Hawaii than in Japan. We
> have an obligation to this country. We are [adopted sons]
> of America. We want to do our part for America.

Thousands of *Nisei* high school and college students mobilized to guard Hawaiian power plants, reservoirs, and waterfronts. "Japan's dastardly attack leaves us grim and resolute.... Japan has chosen to fight us and we'll fight," said Shunzo Sakamaki.

On the evening of December 7 the Korean National Association in Los Angeles pledged its aid to the United States. Members volunteered for the armed forces, purchased war bonds, and wore badges that identified them as Koreans. Ironically, federal officials had declared Koreans citizens of Japan because the Japanese had occupied Korea. Complained one Korean American:

> For years we've been fighting the Japanese, and now they tell us that we're Japs. It's an insult.

By New Year's Day, 1942, 50 Korean Americans had enrolled in the California National Guard. By 1943, Koreans in Hawaii had contributed more than $26 million to the war effort and those on America's mainland more than $240 million. Korean Americans knew the Japanese language, and many volunteered to broadcast America's messages to Japan, translate Japanese documents, and serve as spies in Japanese-held territories. Some taught the Japanese language to U.S. Army recruits. Elderly Korean American women served the Red Cross and elderly men served as air-raid wardens.

Filipino American soldiers fought beside U.S. troops on Bataan Peninsula in the Philippines. To Eleanor Roosevelt, Bataan was

> an excellent example of what happens when two different races respect each other. Men of different races and backgrounds have fought side by side and praised each other's heroism and courage.

In 1943 Congress passed a law that allowed Filipino Americans to become U.S. citizens. And in 1944, a Filipino American, Vincent Lim, Jr., son of a Filipino Army general, graduated from West Point.

About 70,000 Native Americans helped bring victory. In 1945 *Colliers Magazine* noted that 25,000 Native Americans "have served in the armed forces, with the highest volunteering record, we believe, of any population in the country." Navajos in the marines used their native tongue to create a secret battlefield code.

Native Americans earned 34 Distinguished Flying Crosses and two Congressional Medals of Honor. Ernest Childers, a Creek, earned his Medal of Honor fighting in Italy in an all-Indian Oklahoma Company. Marine pilot Pat Flynn, a Rosebud Sioux, was shot down over Japan but managed to evade capture, fly again, and become a colonel. Will Rogers, Jr., whose ancestors included Cherokees, served in the armed forces and later became a special assistant to the commissioner of Indian Affairs.

Leaving reservations to work in defense plants or the armed forces, Native Americans opened a new era and ended their cultural isolation. Maria Tallchief Paschen, an Osage, at 18 joined the Ballet Russe de Monte Carlo in 1942. She later starred with the Paris Opera Company and then the New York City Ballet.

Born in Oklahoma in 1891, Choctaw William Stigler graduated from Northeastern State College in 1912 and served in World War I. In 1944 he was elected to Congress from Oklahoma.

Ira Hayes

Ira Hayes, a Pima, joined the marines as a parachutist. He became famous when he helped raise the U.S. flag at Iwo Jima. But then he returned home and was arrested 50 times for drunkenness and once for escaping from an Arizona work gang. In 1953 at a Flag Day ceremony in Chicago, Hayes said:

> I was out in Arizona for eight years, and nobody paid any attention to me. They might ask me what I think of the way they treat Indians out there, compared to how we are treated in Chicago. I'd tell them the truth, and Arizona would not like it.

Hayes died a poor man in 1955 and was given a hero's funeral. In a Hollywood movie of his life a white actor was cast as Hayes.

Chinese Americans were also striving to be accepted into American society. "To men of my generation," said Charlie Leong, a Chinese American, "World War II was the most important historic event of our times. For the first time we felt we could make it in American society." President Roosevelt called the 1882 Chinese Exclusion Act "a historic mistake." In 1943 he convinced Congress to repeal the act:

> China is our ally. For many long years she stood alone in the fight against aggression. Today we fight at her side.

But the law's real impact was on Chinese Americans. Recalled Harold Liu of New York's Chinatown:

> All of a sudden we became part of the American dream....
> In the community we began to feel very good about ourselves.

A total of 13,499 Chinese American men joined the U.S. armed forces. Chinese American women worked in defense industries. Said Florence Gee, a teenager:

> I am an American…. The war has hit home. I have an
> uncle in the army and one in the shipyard. My sisters are
> members of the civilian defense. My mother is taking first
> aid. I belong to a club where I learn better citizenship.

Polish, Czech, French, British, Latvian, Mexican, Portuguese, Scandinavian, and other ethnic Americans served in the armed forces. Leon Swirbul, promoted to brigadier general, became the highest ranking Latvian American in U.S. military history. He later became president of Grumman Aircraft. About 50,000 Hungarian Americans served in the armed forces, including Mrs. John Hegedus's seven sons. Detroit sent 12 percent of its adult male Hungarian Americans to serve in the armed forces.

On Columbus Day, 1942, President Roosevelt announced that the phrase "enemy aliens" would no longer apply to people who had been born in Italy. Italian Americans had demonstrated their patriotism on every battlefield. Sergeant John Basilone of New Jersey became the first marine enlistee awarded a Congressional Medal of Honor. On the first day of the Guadalcanal invasion he virtually wiped out an enemy regiment, and General MacArthur called him a "one-man army." Basilone died leading his platoon against the Japanese on the Pacific island of Iwo Jima.

About 20,000 Armenian Americans served in the war, and Corporal James Topazian was the first Armenian American killed. The first soldier to die in the invasion of Africa was Armenian American Lt. I. Kousharian. Lt. Ernest Devrishian of Virginia won the Medal of Honor for his bravery during the Italian campaign. Dsaghig and Manishag Aslanian were the first twin sisters to serve in the Women's Army Corps (WAC). The first Armenian American general was Haig Shekerjian, appointed by Roosevelt in 1942.

Several thousand Ukrainian Americans served in the armed forces. Nicholas Minue was awarded the Medal of Honor for his one-man attack on a Nazi machine-gun crew. The first Ukrainian American graduate of West Point, Lt. Colonel Theodore Kalakula, led a daring assault after his company commander was slain.

More than 5,000 Romanian Americans joined the U.S. armed forces including Rudolph Piskuran, who died at Pearl Harbor. Floarea Buzella left her Pennsylvania home to become the first Romanian American to enlist in the WAVES. Lt. Alexandru Vraciu of the Navy Air Force shot down 19 Japanese planes. In 1944 Romanian Americans raised the cash to purchase a Liberty ship which they named for Romanian Civil War hero George Pumutz.

Scandinavians joined the armed forces by the thousands. Major Richard Bong, son of a Swedish immigrant, became America's leading air ace in the Pacific. The Ninth Infantry, a special "Norse Battalion," trained at Fort Snelling, Minnesota, to liberate Norway.

In World War I government propaganda tried to stir hatred against German Americans but not in World War II. More than three million German Americans served in the armed forces. Sergeant Klaus Mann wrote in the army's *Stars and Stripes* and told of:

> our natural loyalty to a new homeland to which we are deeply indebted; and second, our intimate, firsthand knowledge of the moral danger which Hitlerism means to civilization…. We left because we realized that Hitler would inevitably lead the German nation to war, to disgrace, and to disaster.

Herman Bottcher, born in Germany, had been a major in the Lincoln Brigade in Spain. After Pearl Harbor, he enlisted in the American army as a private. In New Guinea, when his superior officers were killed or wounded, Sgt. Bottcher took command of an infantry company. For his daring and bravery, he was awarded a battlefield commission and the Distinguished Service Cross. In 1943 Eleanor Roosevelt asked to meet Bottcher. He died in 1944 while fighting with his men in the Pacific theater.

Herman Bottcher receiving the Distinguished Service Cross.

Mexican Americans in the armed forces numbered 400,000, with a higher percentage of them fighting overseas and receiving military medals than those of any other ethnic group. Many saw combat as a chance to prove their value in ways that discrimination had denied them as civilians. They volunteered as frontline troops and paratroopers and suffered a higher casualty rate than any other ethnic group. A total of 12 Hispanic men earned the Congressional Medal of Honor.

American Jews flocked to the armed forces 550,000 strong, and more than 36,000 received awards for bravery. Jewish American Lincoln Brigade veterans eagerly sought the opportunity to finish the job they began in Spain. George Watt, born to immigrant parents (named Kwatt) in 1912, and a Lincoln Brigade officer, became a machine gunner on an American B-17 over Germany. When his plane was shot down during his seventh mission, Watt parachuted into Nazi-occupied Belgium. Villagers hid him by day and moved him by night through a network run by women. He slipped through Nazi checkpoints in Belgium and France, crossed into Spain, and finally reached safety in British Gibralter. Watt and his wife returned after the war to meet and thank those who helped saved his life and to write the tale of his escape in *The Comet Connection*.

The Office of Strategic Services (OSS — later the CIA) was created by Irish American "Wild Bill" Donovan. Since Americans had no experience behind Nazi lines, Donovan's first experts were veterans of the Lincoln Brigade. "I want all your ideas, everything you learned about guerrilla war and underground operations in Spain," Donovan told the veterans — Jewish Americans Irving Goff, Milton Wolff, Al Tanz, Milton Felsen, and Vince Lossowsky, and Billy Aalto, a Finnish American.

William Donovan began the OSS, which later became the CIA.

Donovan found that in Spain his recruits had made friends of key European antifascist resistance leaders, and their contacts proved invaluable. In North Africa, Goff led a commando raid that liberated a Nazi concentration camp. In Sicily, with help from Italians he knew from Spain, Goff placed 22 American intelligence teams behind enemy lines — and 21 were successful. In northern Italy, Goff's team placed 18 radio teams behind enemy lines:

"Easter eggs" for delivery to Hitler in 1945.

> We had a map of all the German positions. The American army knew where every German was.

Some three million African Americans registered for the draft, but more than one in ten were turned down because they lacked a fourth-grade education. A total of 701,678 African Americans were in the army, 165,000 in the navy, 5,000 in the Coast Guard, 17,000 in the marines, and 4,000 African American women became Wacs and Waves.

Half a million African Americans served overseas. But due to discrimination 71 percent were confined to quartermaster, engineer, or transportation duties rather than combat units. In the navy 95 percent of all African Americans remained in the messmate classification. Until 1943, the marines had never accepted a black man but had enlisted 17,000 by the war's end.

Secretary of War Henry Stimson echoed an old army belief when he stated that African Americans could not be turned into "really effective combat troops without all officers being white." People of color had to fight for the right to be trained as officers for the army and the air force.

Army general Benjamin Davis and heavyweight boxing champion Joe Louis during World War II.

After pressure from civil rights organizations, the air force accepted and trained African American officers. Colonel Benjamin O. Davis, Jr., son of America's first black general Benjamin O. Davis, commanded the 332nd Fighter Group that flew hundreds of missions in the skies over Italy and Germany. For an air attack on Berlin, the 332nd won the highest unit citation.

In the Battle of the Bulge in December 1944, when Nazi forces broke through Allied defenses, the lines of American segregation suddenly dissolved. The U.S. Army quickly recruited and sent 2,500 black soldiers into the First Army's counterattack. But segregation was restored again after the Nazi surrender.

Black men fought in every theater of operations. In April 1945, the 761st Battalion, the only African American tank unit in the U.S. Army, liberated the Nazi death camps at Buchenwald and Dachau. Guards were machine-gunning Jewish prisoners at Buchenwald, so the 761st opened fire and then entered the camp. Sergeant Bill McBurney, commanding the 761st Batallion, recalled:

> You might be trained for combat. But nobody was trained for what we saw. I never saw anything like that. They [surviving prisoners] were skin and bones. My men and I got out and started to hand them food.

"They were our saviors," recalled Abe Chapinick. Writer Elie Wiesel, one of the rescued, later recalled his liberation:

"The most moving moment of my life was the day the Americans arrived, a few hours after the SS had fled…. I will always remember with love a big black soldier. He was crying like a child — tears of all the pain in the world and all the rage. Everyone who was there that day will forever feel a sentiment of gratitude to the American soldiers who liberated us."

Black troops of the 761st Tank Battalion were the liberators of Buchenwald and Dachau, Nazi concentration camps.

Dr. Charles Drew

Born in 1904 to an African American father and mother, Charles Drew was the oldest of five children. Six feet tall, solidly built, he became a four-letter athlete in high school sports. A scholarship student at Amherst College, he became an outstanding athlete and received a trophy as the most valuable football player. Discrimination, however, kept him from being chosen team captain. He also had to work as a waiter to supplement his meager scholarship funds.

At McGill University in Canada, Drew obtained a degree in medicine and began research into blood plasma and transfusions. He developed blood banks that saved the lives of British soldiers in World War II. Later he became the director of the American Red Cross Blood Bank in New York City and used his position to publicly denounce the practice of segregating blood according to the race of the donor. Meanwhile, Drew's plasma system saved the lives of countless American soldiers of all races.

Driving to a medical conference in 1950, Drew's car crashed near Burlington, North Carolina. Drew bled to death before he could reach a hospital. ■

CHAPTER 3

FIGHTING FOR FREEDOM ON THE HOME FRONT

As American armies fought Fascism overseas in the name of democracy, people of color and women saw World War II as an opportunity to advance toward equality and justice on the home front. The struggle was often frustrating and uphill. Segregation remained the law of the land throughout the country and in the armed forces. Major universities and many corporations had quotas that prevented or limited the entrance or hiring of Jewish or African Americans. Most country clubs barred people of color, Hispanics, and Jews from club membership.

During the war, the U.S. home front was not at peace. Eighteen African Americans were lynched. Thirty AFL unions openly denied membership to Blacks. By refusing to vote it funds, Congress ended the Fair Employment Practices Commission at the war's end.

Black soldiers faced white rioters in southern bases. In Alexandria, Louisiana, 28 black servicemen were shot by civilians and white army officers. In Salina, Kansas, when black troops were denied service in a restaurant that fed Nazi prisoners of war, black orientation officer Lloyd Brown urged his men not to despair.

> If we were *untermenschen* in Nazi Germany, they would break our bones. As "colored" men in Salina, they only break our hearts.

Despite setbacks, the war against Nazi racism stimulated the thirst for equality. At Fort Devens, Massachusetts, in 1945 four African American Wacs fought racism and were arrested for insubordination. In Freeman Field, Indiana, 101 black flying officers were arrested for protesting a segregated officers' club.

Resistance to racism sometimes scored impressive gains. In New York a four-month boycott of city buses led to the hiring of black drivers and mechanics. In the center of Chicago, the Congress of Racial Equality (CORE) staged its first sit-in demonstration and desegregated a diner.

African Americans won new election victories. In 1943 Illinois Democrat William Dawson was elected to the U.S. Congress. He became the first person of color to serve as vice president of his party's central committee. In New York City Benjamin Davis, a Communist, won a seat on the city council in 1943 and was reelected two years later. Adam Clayton Powell, Jr., a Baptist minister, in 1945 became the first man of color to represent Harlem in Congress and served for a quarter century.

Congressman William Dawson

Mexican Americans also used the war to gain new footholds in the United States. The U.S. and Mexico agreed to a "bracero program" that encouraged Mexicans to leave their homeland and take farm jobs in the American Southwest. The first braceros reached Stockton, California, on railroad cars bearing the slogan "De Las Democracias Sera la Victoria." As they brought in crops, each was paid $16.50 a week and sometimes as little as $550 a year. Factory jobs opened that had once been closed to Mexican Americans, and their wages rose during the war.

Adam Clayton Powell, Jr., in 1942.

In Texas, braceros found they could not go to churches and nightclubs, were denied burial in "white" cemeteries, and had to send their children to segregated schools. The Mexican paper *Mañana* commented:

> The Nazis of Texas are not political partners of the *Führer*
> of Germany, but indeed they are slaves to the same
> prejudices and superstitions.

In Los Angeles, braceros were barred from theaters, restaurants, parks, and schools. A sign at a city-owned swimming pool read, "Tuesdays reserved for Negroes and Mexicans."

Violence against Mexicans was common and went unpunished. Novelist Hart Stilwell wrote, "The Mexican knows that he may be killed with impunity by any American who chooses to kill him."

At one point Mexico halted the bracero migration to protest racial violence. It also requested protective laws for its citizens. To avoid the law, Texas farm owners knowingly hired "wetbacks" — workers who illegally crossed the border for jobs.

Even decorated war heroes became victims of racism. Sergeant José Mendoza was awarded the Congressional Medal of Honor and sent on a goodwill tour of Mexico by the U.S. Army. He returned home to Texas and was denied service in a diner. When Sgt. Macario García, Medal of Honor recipient, asked for a cup of coffee in Texas, he was told, "We don't serve Mexicans."

Soon after Pearl Harbor, the media and lawmen in California created a "Mexican crime wave." A Los Angeles police report stated that Mexican American juvenile delinquents had a "desire to kill, or at least let blood." Nazi radio stations used portions of the report to prove that Americans really accepted Hitler's racist doctrines.

Trouble between the Los Angeles police and the Mexican American community began in 1942 when police arrested 600 teenagers in August alone. Young Mexican Americans had become increasingly frustrated with teachers who mocked their language, culture, and abilities. Once out of school, they were barred from learning trades and offered low-paying jobs. To increase family income, many left school for farm jobs. One student recalled:

> Lots of kids that go to pick the fruits get behind from school, or sometimes you wait until the next term comes. But then you forget how to talk good English 'cause you only talk Mexican at home. Or maybe you don't go back 'cause the teacher call you dumb Mex — 'cause nobody's got time to help you, there's too many kids late from the crops. So a lot of kids quit and start hunting jobs.

They had received enough education to alienate them from their parents and not enough to make a decent living, so many young Mexican Americans joined gangs. The media began to describe the young men as "pachucos" or "zoot-suiters," a reference to their fancy clothes. The Los Angeles district attorney announced that "zoot suits are an open indication of subversive character."

In June 1943, the first of the "Zoot Suit Riots" pitted Mexican American youths against U.S. soldiers and sailors. A Mexican American of 19 said, "Everybody was against us — the police most of all. So what could we do but fight?"

A white mob surged into downtown Los Angeles and assaulted anyone wearing a "zoot suit" or who had a dark skin. The L.A.

Police helped by arresting "zoot-suiters." The rioting ended only after U.S. military police and the navy shore patrol restored order. The L.A. police and the media denied the violence was racial.

Riots marked 1943. In Detroit in the spring a riot began after white workers struck the Packard auto plant to protest the hiring of African Americans. In one day 34 people were killed, mostly African Americans, 17 of whom died at the hands of white police. President Roosevelt sent 6,000 federal troops to Detroit.

Detroit erupted in antiblack rioting in 1943.

In May a riot erupted in a Mobile, Alabama, shipyard when African American workers were upgraded and assigned to work with whites. In June, when white rioters in Beaumont, Texas, invaded a black neighborhood, it took martial law to restore order.

In August, Harlem, New York, faced a new kind of racial outburst. African Americans rioted against police brutality. Five people were killed and 400 injured before 8,000 National Guard troops and 6,600 city police and volunteers restored order. The riot led to hiring more African American police officers for Harlem.

White ethnic groups used the war against Fascism to push into the mainstream. The war further accelerated assimilation since it stressed the patriotic need to unite against Fascism. In 1942 more than 90 percent of Norwegian American church services were held in English, and this trend continued throughout the nation in other ethnic churches.

At the same time, national unity led to new opportunities. Dr. Ann Dumitru of Pennsylvania and Dr. Eleanor Botha of Minnesota became the first women physicians of Romanian American descent. Frank Oliveira, born to immigrants from the Azores, was elected to the Massachusetts state legislature in 1944. He was the first elected Portuguese American and served until 1958.

The war advanced democracy at home. More discrimination cases were brought before state and federal courts than ever before. In 1943 New York State passed a law that banned discrimination and provided fines and jail for violators. New York said it would prosecute hotels and resorts that used the word "restricted" — meaning a refusal to admit Jewish and African American guests.

A black picket in Chicago in 1942 demands equal rights.

Congressmen Arthur Mitchell sued the Pullman Company for racial discrimination and won his case before the Supreme Court.

Important political figures contrasted America's multiethnicity with Nazi racism. Republican leader Wendell Willkie's *One World* denounced "Our Imperialisms at Home" and said racism impeded the war effort. The CIO announced that the just demands of people of color were a vital part of their program for America. Finally, in a case brought by the NAACP, the Supreme Court found unconstitutional a law in Texas prohibiting people of color from voting in party primaries.

The war gave women an unprecedented chance to assume new roles. In May 1942, Congress created the Women's Army Corps (WAC) to replace soldiers who could be sent into combat. Colonel Oveta Culp Hobby became its director, and she later served in President Dwight Eisenhower's cabinet.

Eventually, more than a quarter of a million women served as nurses or joined the WAC, WAVES, SPARS, and women marines — women's auxiliaries to branches of the armed services.

U.S. Wacs receiving tear gas training at Scott Field, Illinois, in 1943.

Women had to be between 20 and 49, American citizens, and without any children under 14. They had to have good health, a good character, and at least two years of high school or similar educational experience. Wacs served as typists, cashiers, chauffeurs, radio operators, and bakers. The air force trained women pilots. The military services, however, did not place women in positions where they could give orders to men, and the services kept them from serving overseas until the last two years of the war. Black women were segregated in these services.

About three million women joined the Red Cross to work in hospitals, canteens, motor corps, and to recruit nurses. Others served in civilian defense and for the United Service Organizations (USO).

The war dramatically changed job opportunities for women. Work considered "unsuited to women" in peacetime suddenly became jobs they should take as a patriotic duty. In the first six months after Pearl Harbor, employers raised from 29 percent to 55 percent the proportion of positions open to women.

By 1944, women made up a third of the civilian work force — 18,150,000 people. This became a revolutionary change because six million of the women had never held jobs before, and many were married. For the first time American women began to dominate certain fields such as clerical work and teaching.

Half a million women worked in the aircraft industry. The number of women working in metal, chemical, and rubber plants increased over 460 percent between 1939 and 1944. Shipyards once had barred women, but now female employees were a tenth of the work force.

"Rosie the Riveter" became a popular hero. Pretty women in dungarees and work clothes were portrayed in ads seeking defense plant laborers. War work, women were assured, did not undermine their femininity. But their pay was less than half of what men received.

Black women found new opportunities they had been denied in peacetime industry but had to work at lower wages than white women. Even so, in the war years half of African American women in farm work left to take new jobs in cities.

During the war, union membership for women rose from 800,000 to 3 million, and the female proportion in unions rose from 11 percent to 23 percent. The presence of women spurred union activism. In Detroit in 1942 and 1943, African American women members of the United Auto Workers demonstrated for jobs and housing with the support of their union. More than a hundred of these black women stormed a Ford factory to protest discrimination.

World War II's Literacy Training Program

In 1942 the U.S. Army turned down 340,000 able-bodied recruits for reasons of illiteracy. The next year it initiated a program to train 185,000 Americans to read and write and hired instructors from the ranks of whites and people of color.

The program was a huge success. Eighty-five percent, or 150,000 men, including 86,670 people of color, became literate. The white success rate was 84.2 percent and for Blacks, 87.1 percent. The final report was celebrated as the "greatest experiment of its kind ever conducted by the American government." The results, it also pointed out, "constitute a shattering blow to racists." ∎

CHAPTER 4

JAPANESE AMERICANS: FROM INTERNEES TO SOLDIERS

In 1942 Japanese Americans are evacuated from the state of Washington to relocation camps in California.

Japan's attack on Pearl Harbor unleashed waves of American racial animosity toward Japanese Americans. FBI agents searched hundreds of Japanese American homes and arrested 1,370 people. The Treasury Department froze Japanese American bank accounts, and the U.S. Army discharged soldiers born in Japan.

Though no acts of sabotage took place, on the West Coast, curfews were imposed on Japanese Americans. No similar actions were taken against German or Italian Americans.

The worst was yet to come. Boards of Supervisors in 16 California counties warned about "another Pearl Harbor" inside the country and called for the detention of all Japanese Americans — the *Issei*, those born abroad, and the *Nisei*, those born in the United States. Attorney General Earl Warren said Japanese Americans "may well be the Achilles heel of the civilian defense effort." U.S. Army general John De Witt claimed that "the Japanese race is an enemy race" since "its racial strains are undiluted."

Whites used this government hysteria to take over Japanese American farms. Austin Anson of the Grower-Shipper Vegetable Association said his society "wanted to get rid of the Japs for selfish reasons."

In February 1942, President Roosevelt, using his war powers, issued Executive Order No. 9066 against espionage and sabotage, which established "relocation camps" for people of Japanese ancestry. Some Japanese Americans felt relief at the decision. "People were getting their houses burned down, and we were afraid those things might happen to us," recalled Mrs. Margaret Takahashi, a mother of three.

Families were given from 48 hours to two weeks to leave. "You could only take one suitcase apiece," said Mrs. Takahashi. "I remember how agonizing was my despair," said Tom Hayase, "to be given only about six days in which to dispose of my property." Whites arrived to buy homes and land, said one evacuee, and "we had no recourse but to accept whatever they were offering."

About 110,000 men, women, and children were held in barbed-wire enclosed camps in Arizona, Utah, Colorado, California, Idaho, Arkansas, and Wyoming. A camp in New Jersey imprisoned people from the East Coast. No internee had committed any crime.

Two-thirds of those imprisoned were American citizens who had come to love America. Robert Matsui later recalled:

> How could I, as a six-month-old child born in this country, be declared by my own government to be an enemy alien?

A Japanese American about to leave for a relocation camp shows his land and crop to white buyers in April 1942 near Los Angeles.

Japanese Americans found living conditions and work in the camps regimented and boring but not oppressive. Inmates shared the same kind of food, clothes, barracks, showers, and bathrooms. Illiterate and highly educated inmates performed the some jobs. Families, allowed to plant their own gardens, did this with loving care.

However, internment divided prisoners. The Japanese American Citizens' League (JACL) represented the majority and urged compliance with all rules. Opposing them were the *Kibei*, the nine percent of young people edu-

At internment camps Japanese Americans elected governing councils.

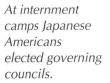

cated in Japan who were furious at internment and wanted to return "home." The *Issei* often clashed with the *Nisei*. Internees who collaborated with or befriended guards were disdained as *inu*, or "dog."

Camp administrators did not allow the celebration of Japanese holidays and discouraged the use of the Japanese language and customs. Some inmates staged strikes to oppose camp authority.

Hawaii offered a sharp contrast to the mainland. The island's Japanese Americans were a third of the total population, but there were no internment camps or hysteria. Hawaiians knew that a roundup of people would cripple their economy and war effort.

In October 1942, Tokyo radio propaganda used the internment of Japanese Americans to prove to other Asians that the United States was fighting "a racial war." The President began to change his policies. In February 1943, FDR opened the U.S. armed forces to interned Japanese citizens. "Americanism is not, and never was," FDR said, "a matter of race or ancestry."

Internees were allowed to leave the camps but only if they could find work in other parts of the country. Internee Mitsuye Endo sued for her freedom. A government employee, she tested the constitutionality of being interned without a trial. In 1944 the U.S. Supreme Court agreed with her and ended the internment camps.

The U.S. Army started to recruit in the camps in 1942 and found that only 1,250 of 10,000 eligible volunteered. Dunks Oshima said, "What do they take us for? Saps?" In Hawaii, however, tens of thousands of Japanese Americans volunteered for the army.

In all, 33,000 Japanese Americans served in the armed forces, demonstrating their obligations as citizens and their loyalty to America. One family sent nine sons to various armed services. Ben Kuroki left his internment camp for the U.S. Air Force and flew 30 bombing missions in Europe. After his B-24 was shot down, and he escaped internment in Spanish Morocco, he requested Pacific duty. He took part in 28 other bombing missions against Japan. General George Marshall and four other U.S. generals asked to be introduced to Sergeant Kuroki.

Richard Sakakida's translation of Japan's secret plans made it possible for the Americans to ambush their Bataan landing. In Burma, Japanese American recruits, reported a white officer, "crawled up close enough to be able to hear... officers' commands and to make verbal translations to our soldiers." "Never before in history," said Major General Charles Willoughby, "did an army know so much concerning its enemy, prior to actual engagements, as did the American army during most of the Pacific campaigns."

In June 1944, the famed Japanese American 442nd "Go for Broke" Division landed in Italy and fought at Luciana, Livorno, and the Arno River. A fourth of the men were killed or wounded. In France's Vosges Mountains they rescued 211 men from a Texas battalion. "We were never so glad to see anyone as those fighting Japanese Americans," said one survivor.

The 442nd became the most decorated unit in the U.S. Army, with 18,143 individual awards. Of 33,000 men, 9,486 were wounded, and 6,000 died. In Italy, Captain Daniel Inouye was about to throw a grenade when a rifle-grenade destroyed his right arm. His left hand snatched the grenade from his right fist, threw it at a Nazi soldier,

A Young Voice from the Camp

On file at the Bancroft Library, University of California at Berkeley, is this young Japanese American's statement about his internment.

I simply cannot sleep nights — thinking of the injustice of everything.

As an American, I revolt because it was my understanding that we were sacrificing our homes, our life that we had worked and planned for our children and ourselves — as a patriotic duty, evacuating for military reasons and all such reasons which I question now. I challenge any American to stack up their record against any of us and see if we hadn't been as good or better Americans in deed and to think today — we and our children (third and fourth generation Americans — who have to live in this country after this mess is over) have to be confined in concentration camps. If we are to really be victorious fighting for the preservation of democracy and the American way of life, we had better review the constitutionality of all this right here in the U.S.A. If we feel this way now — I wonder how we will feel in two years or three years hence. Really when I see small children and growing youngsters — I can't stand this life. ■

and he then charged ahead "firing my tommy gun left-handed, the useless right arm slapping red and wet against my side."

Back in San Francisco, however, Captain Inouye, his army jacket covered with medals, went for a haircut and was told, "We don't serve Japs here." He later became a United States senator from Hawaii.

In California, Japanese Americans experienced 36 acts of racial violence. And after their release from the internment camps, 8,000 people decided to leave for Japan.

The Takahashi family moved back to Los Angeles after the war and had suppressed their bitterness. Margaret Takahashi recalled:

> From then on we were very strong. I don't think anything could get us down now.

Over the next several decades, the American government tried to make amends. In 1991 Congress offered each internee a compensation of $20,000.

The Rights of Minorities

In the 19th century a religious sect, Jehovah's Witnesses, united around the belief that the Second Coming of Christ was in progress and that it promised redemption for everyone. Jehovah's Witnesses operated without churches or ministers and gathered in buildings they referred to as "New Kingdom."

The Bible, insisted the sect's leaders, did not allow members to salute any flag. Other citizens called this disloyal, and in 1940 the U.S. Supreme Court ruled that compulsory flag salutes in public schools were constitutional. During World War II, criminal actions were brought by some states against parents, and some schoolchildren were expelled for refusing to salute the flag.

In 1943 Jehovah's Witnesses again took their case to the high court. Wrote Justice Robert Jackson for the court majority:

> If there is any fixed star in our constitutional constellation, it is that no official, high or petty, can prescribe what shall be orthodox in politics, nationalism, religion, or other matters of opinion, or force citizens to confess by words or act their faith therein.

Jehovah's Witnesses had won a victory for freedom of religion for all Americans. ■

C H A P T E R 5

POSTWAR WOMEN

At the end of World War II, "Rosie the Riveter" lost her job. In the four months between Nazi Germany's defeat in June and the Japanese surrender in September 1945, one out of every four women quit or was fired. By 1947, five million women had left their jobs.

There were several reasons for this. First, returning veterans wanted their old jobs back, and that seemed the patriotic option. Second, although working women had made victory possible, they had been raised to think of marriage and home ahead of work. Lastly, women who preferred a career to marriage after the war were pictured as maladjusted and less feminine. Ferdinand Lundberg and Marynia Farnham wrote a book in 1947, *Modern Woman: The Lost Sex* to claim that women became "psychologically disordered" when they left the home for a job. They were speaking about white women, since half of America's women of color found work necessary to support their families.

Many women resented being treated as merely a wartime labor force, and some joined picket lines to demand their jobs back. However, most factories refused to hire them, and those that did offered half the pay they earned during the war. An Employment Service officer said to women who had worked in heavy industry during the war, "No, these jobs are for men; women can't do them."

There was no doubt that the war had spurred women to new heights and opened new doors. Eleven states adopted "equal pay for equal work" laws. So did many unions. And it was no longer possible to talk about world human rights without mentioning women and children.

However, the levels of achievement reached by ordinary working women came under attack after the war. Women's magazines

Rubber Workers Union in Buffalo, New York, swearing in new members in 1945.

31

defined "female" to mean a person who marries, stays at home, and raises a family. This drive for conformity had a personal impact on many women. By 1950, women aged 15 to 19 were getting married more than any other age group, and half of all women were married by 20 — new records for marriageable ages.

This pattern continued into the next decade. By 1959, 14 million women were engaged by age 17. Once married, they were twice as likely to have more than three children than women who were married a generation earlier.

Soon 60 percent of women dropped out of college to marry. Since an educated woman was believed less likely to get married, fewer women attended college than in the 1920s. By 1958, five women's colleges had closed down, and 21 had become coed. Anthropologist Margaret Mead found that both men and women were "confused, uncertain, and discontented with the present definition of women's place in America."

In this age of conformity, women's organizations lost their reform focus and their former spirited defense of women's issues. The campaign for an Equal Rights Amendment (ERA) to the Constitution, strong before the war, faded. During the war, white women's societies talked of fighting racial discrimination and accepting people of color as members. Peace ended the discussion, and groups moved on to other matters. When Mary McLeod Bethune tried to organize a coalition of women to combat racism, major white societies decided not to join her.

Mary McLeod Bethune, advisor to Presidents Truman and Roosevelt and civil rights activist.

As the cold war between the United States and the Soviet Union heated up, a woman's role as homemaker was given a political dimension. The housewife was more than someone who cleaned, cooked, and took care of children. She also represented a force against communism. She was pictured as a sentinel guarding the American family, which was portrayed as a bastion against a foe said to lack religion and family values. With women at the helm, it was said, American families had the "togetherness" to combat Soviet Russia and any "communist subversion" in the United States.

At the same time women's domestic role was praised, their role in politics shrunk. Women held less than five percent of public offices. A handful served in Congress or in high appointive office in federal or state governments. No more than one at a time ever served in a presidential cabinet. No one suggested that a woman might make a good president or vice president of the United States.

As time went on, however, in spite of these apparently regressive statistics, some women quietly pursued their own agendas. While white women comprised only 17 percent of workers in 1950, this figure rose to 30 percent in 1960, almost half of labor's growth during the decade. In this economy, service jobs appropriate for women increased while industrial jobs traditionally reserved for men decreased.

While white women's organizations became more conforming and less daring, women of color had to develop a different agenda. In 1950 when Mexican American zinc miners in New Mexico went on strike, their wives asked them to demand better housing. At first the men refused to accept this "female" issue. However, a court injunction forbade men to picket, and the company brought in strikebreakers. Women, some with babies, took over picket lines and fought off "scabs" while the men stayed at home to take care of the children. Even when women pickets were jailed, they remained spirited enough to demand milk for their babies. The Mexican American community learned from the daring of its women. The movie *Salt of the Earth* immortalized their tale.

By means of their churches and participation in urban societies, African American women also began to move into the political arena. African American women worked outside their homes, an increasing number of them as teachers. The lesson they drew from the war was that a better life was there for the taking, and as teachers and mothers they increasingly instilled this in their young. A new generation was taught to resist violence and to demand education and a chance for themselves and their children.

African American women hand out leaflets calling for federal protection of black citizens in southern states.

Women on the Cutting Edge

Meridel Le Sueur, born in 1900 in Iowa of French American parents, had a life of exciting activities and quiet writing. Her mother was an early suffragist and her father was the Socialist mayor of Minot, North Dakota.

Le Sueur dropped out of high school and traveled to New York City, where she acted in the theater and lived in an anarchist commune. Later, in Hollywood, she took a job as a movie stuntwoman.

In the 1930s, Le Sueur became a novelist who saw herself as the "voice, messenger, and awakener" of the oppressed, particularly women. In 1936 she participated with many famous authors of the day in the first American Writers Congress.

Le Sueur also helped organize the unemployed and dispossessed. In the 1950s she had trouble finding publishers or keeping a job. When the feminist movement grew in the 1970s, her early works were reprinted, and she became one of its role models. In 1981 she and Toni Morrison were the two keynote speakers at a new National Writers Congress.

Audley Moore, born into an African American family in Louisiana in 1898, had completed just three years of formal education. She became an ardent supporter of black leader Marcus Garvey and in 1919 recruited an armed black force to protect Garvey's right to speak in New Orleans. She then left for New York City to work in his campaigns.

Moore became a Communist and in 1938 the party's candidate for state assembly. In 1940 she ran for the office of alderman. She left the Communist Party in 1950 for the politics of black nationalism. She and her sister formed the Universal Association of Ethiopian Women to protest lynchings in the South. She tutored the young Malcolm Little, who became Malcolm X. In 1963 she established a reparations committee to demand compensation for all whose ancestors had been enslaved. When South African freedom-fighter Nelson Mandela, after 26 years in jail, visited Harlem in 1991, "Queen Mother" Moore welcomed him at the airport and introduced him to Harlem.

Rachel Carson, born in 1907 in Pennsylvania, got her M.A. from Johns Hopkins University in 1932 and became a marine biologist. She wrote three books on sea life.

Carson began to investigate the harm that people, especially in the industrialized nations, were inflicting on the Earth's food and water by using chemical methods to control pests and insects. She was shocked by what she found and felt she had no choice but to sound an alarm. Her book *Silent Spring*, published in 1962, detailed the detrimental effect insecticides had on the human food supply and the environment. It ushered in an era of concern for the environment. Carson died in her fifties only two years after the book was published. ∎

CHAPTER 6

ELEANOR ROOSEVELT

The United States has had many First Ladies, and some of them have been remembered fondly for their contributions to the nation. Eleanor Roosevelt's contribution was in a class by itself.

Born in 1884 to a famous and rich American family, Eleanor's father was President Theodore Roosevelt's brother. But life was not easy for young Eleanor, whose mother died when she was eight followed by her father the next year. She grew up feeling she was ugly and, at nearly six feet, too tall. Until age 15, she had no friends of her own.

When Eleanor married Franklin Delano Roosevelt, a distant cousin, in 1905, the wedding was in the White House and President Teddy Roosevelt gave the bride away. She cut her own energetic path through society's demands. She did little housework — "fifteen minutes a day," she once said — and became deeply involved in reform movements and women's issues.

In 1920 her husband was defeated when he ran for vice president of the United States. The next year Franklin came down with polio, and the couple determined this would not be another defeat. Eleanor would be his eyes and ears. He was elected governor of New York, and she was there as his political helpmate. But her personal life was not easy, for their marriage had come apart years before, and they lived virtually separate lives.

When Franklin D. Roosevelt was elected President of the United States in 1932, she was everywhere for him. Each year Eleanor Roosevelt covered 40,000 miles of the United States lecturing, listening, and visiting slums, sharecroppers' homes, and schools. In Roosevelt's first year as president, Eleanor called the first press conference ever held by a First Lady. Two years later she began writing a weekly news column, "My Day," which appeared in 135 papers. She held a press conference once a week for women reporters and often appeared on radio interview programs.

Eleanor Roosevelt in 1943 visited a black orphanage in Riverdale, NY.

President Roosevelt's enemies hated Eleanor even more than they did him. He was "that man in the White House," and she was angrily called "Her!" Eleanor's views were more radical than Franklin's. She stood up against racial and religious bigotry in public again and again. She infuriated certain senators by being photographed with people of color, the jobless, and the homeless. During World War II, she visited war-torn England in 1942 and Pacific battlefields in 1943 — and served as the national head of Russian War Relief.

Eleanor Roosevelt always seemed on the side of the persecuted. During the cold war, when it was politically dangerous to do so, she defended the rights of Communists. No congressional "red-hunting" committee dared call her to testify because she was too opinionated and popular.

Winston Churchill told her the best way to keep peace in the world was through a strong military alliance. She answered that a better way would be to improve everyone's living standards.

After FDR died in 1945, Eleanor continued with her crusades for children, peace, consumer welfare, and civil rights. She served as a U.S. delegate to the United Nations from 1946 to 1953. At the UN she became the person most responsible for the passage of its famous Declaration of Human Rights. She favored an Equal Rights Amendment to the Constitution. Her final triumph was to serve as chair for President Kennedy's Commission on Women that called for new laws to protect women. She died in 1962 just before the final report was issued.

CHAPTER 7

THE LONG RED SCARE

World War I was followed by a Red (Communist) Scare, and World War II was followed by a cold war in which "Reds" once again became objects of fear and loathing. This second Red Scare lasted for decades, and it touched every aspect of American life.

Politicians again played on the popular fear of Russian communism to claim that Reds and other "subversives" were about to overthrow the government. Leaders of the tiny Communist Party were brought to trial for "advocating the forcible overthrow" of the government, and hundreds were sent to jail.

Most anticommunists cared little about Communists or Russians. Their targets were those Democrats who had favored New Deal programs and had believed that the wartime alliance with the USSR should continue in peace. Anticommunists went after Americans who believed in strong unions, racial integration, housing for the poor, and a program of national health care.

Some politicians used the Red Scare to restrict the Bill of Rights and to impose narrow views of morality on the public. Almost any man or woman who differed with official government positions could be accused of communism and possibly lose a job.

People who spoke for racial integration or independence for women first had to explain that they were not Communists. Once accused of being Reds, people found they were denied access to radio, TV, and community audiences.

This attitude characterized by baseless charges and political hysteria has been named "McCarthyism" after Senator Joseph McCarthy, who was perhaps the loudest of the anticommunists. But McCarthy stumbled upon the magical power of anticommunism in 1950, years after others had used it. The House Un-American Activities Committee (HUAC) in the 1930s had played on Red fears to smear President and Eleanor Roosevelt, the New Deal, labor unions, racial minorities, and a host of reforms.

Anticommunist fanatics came from every class and ethnic group, and so did their victims. Any accused person was allowed to clear his or her name by declaring oneself an anticommunist. Some foreigners were deported because they had briefly joined the Communist Party during World War II. Australian-born Harry Bridges faced years of court efforts to revoke his citizenship for having associated with "known Communists." Charlie Chaplin went to live in Europe rather than face questions about his beliefs. Famous scientists such as Robert Oppenheimer were declared security risks and lost their jobs.

The FBI kept files on the political views of millions of ordinary and famous Americans. To save their jobs, civil servants, movie stars, teachers, and librarians had to tell government committees about their private political views and associations.

Racist politicians used anticommunism to smear anyone who challenged white supremacy and discrimination. Reds opposed segregation and favored equality, so civil rights groups and leaders were constantly accused of subversion. The Red hysteria wrecked the careers of African Americans such as the popular actor Paul Robeson and the noted scholar W. E. B. Du Bois.

As many as 2,000 seaman were screened off the waterfront. When Captain Hugh Mulzac of the *Booker T. Washington* was called "a security risk" for Coast Guard work, he demanded a hearing.

Paul Robeson, Dr. W.E.B. Du Bois, and New York congressman Vito Marcantonio, who served as Du Bois' attorney free of charge. All three challenged McCarthyism.

I was dumbfounded. I had risked my life countless times during World War I and World War II in the service of my country. I had never knowingly been connected with any organization plotting its overthrow by force and violence.

Mulzac was asked whom he associated with, what papers he read, what public rallies he attended, and why his *Washington* crew praised Soviet Russia's military effort in World War II. He was asked why he joined interracial groups and tried to promote equality in the United States and freedom in the West Indies and Africa. Finally, Mulzac, who was dismissed from the Coast Guard, said:

There were no witnesses against me... [The charges] could have come from a neighbor who disliked me.

Steve Nelson (born Masarosh) came to America from Yugoslavia as a boy in 1919. He and his wife Margaret, a German American, became members of the Communist Party. During the depression, Nelson led Unemployment Councils, and fought for unions and against racism. In 1933 Steve and Margaret went to school in the USSR. They each entered Nazi Germany twice to aid underground fighters arrayed against Hitler. In 1937 Steve Nelson became a commander of the Lincoln Brigade in Spain. Judging by their record the Nelsons might have been considered heroes in the fight against Fascism. But Steve Nelson was a Communist, had visited the USSR, and had briefly befriended Oppenheimer before the war. So in 1949 he was accused of being a "Soviet spy master."

Steve Nelson (left) returned to Spain triumphantly in 1986 where he was greeted by Spanish general Lister and U.S. writer Marc Crawford.

In three trials in 1950 and 1951, Nelson was tried and convicted of "advocating" the overthrow of the government. In one trial he could not even find an attorney willing to handle his case and had to become, with Margaret's help, his own attorney.

The only evidence against Nelson was his collection of 300 books on communism. The prosecutor called these books "more dangerous than guns." A jury agreed, and he was sentenced to 20 years in jail.

From the beginning, Nelson and many others who stood up to the hysteria paid a high price. Some people committed suicide. Italian American Congressman Vito Marcantonio, who defended Communists' rights in court was, after serving six terms, defeated for reelection when the two major parties united against him.

Few in Congress dared challenge the Red Scare, but Senator Margaret Chase Smith, Maine's first congresswoman, denounced Senator McCarthy's smear tactics as un-American. Smith was one of the few to fight McCarthy without ruining her political career.

Some victims of the Red Scare bravely invoked their First Amendment rights to free speech and association. Playwright Lillian Hellman told HUAC she would never "tailor my beliefs to the current political fashion." Actor Zero Mostel, son of a rabbi, told HUAC if they wanted to fight un-American activities they

Playwright Lillian Hellman (top) and playwright Arthur Miller (left) dared to challenge the Red hunters.

should start with themselves. Scholar William Mandel called McCarthy a murderer since the senator's hounding of a young scientist had led the man to commit suicide.

McCarthy, who was censured by the Senate in 1955, died a few years later. Other politicians carried on the hysteria, but they found mounting resistance from the public and the courts.

Some victims won their rights back. Paul Robeson's passport was taken away by the government, and this ended his singing and acting career. When he was not allowed to travel to Canada for a concert, he had to sing by telephone. Robeson sued to regain his passport, and the Supreme Court agreed with him. Steve Nelson also carried his case to the high court and won.

By 1962, HUAC faced women who would not cower when accused of communism. When leaders of Women Strike for Peace (WSP) were summoned, they packed the court with hundreds of women and babies. When the audience stood in silent solidarity with the first witness, the chairman forbade anyone to stand up. Witnesses took the Fifth Amendment on almost every question asked, and the audience applauded their defiance. Then applause was outlawed. So women next rushed up to kiss brave witnesses.

When asked about communism, one WSP witness said, "This movement was inspired and motivated by mothers' love for children." By the third day, the crowd gave standing ovations to their heroes without fear of punishment. WSP founder Dagmar Wilson, dressed in red, was confident as she confronted the committee. When she was asked if she would allow a Communist to become a leader of WSP, she answered:

> I would like to say that unless everybody in the whole
> world joins us in the fight, then God help us!

The cold war hysteria began to fade in the 1960s. But many ordinary people had lost their jobs, and some spent time in jail. The Bill of Rights had been violated in the name of national defense. Foreign-born citizens had been classified as "dangerous aliens" and deported to nations they had left as infants. Women's groups, and racial and ethnic organizations had to spend funds to prove their loyalty and purge "Reds" instead of promoting their programs.

CHANGING PATTERNS OF IMMIGRATION

Immigration policies slowly began to relax after World War II from the strict quota systems enacted by Congress in the 1920s. In the War Brides Act of 1946, Congress waived the quotas to admit 120,000 spouses and children of American soldiers who had served overseas. The next year Congress again waived its quotas so that wives of Chinese and Japanese Americans could join their husbands in the United States.

Meanwhile, Congress, in recognition of the war contributions of India and the Philippines, lifted the ban on immigration from these nations and allowed each to send 105 people a year. Japan was also granted a quota of 105 immigrants a year.

The arrival of European and Asian women married to American soldiers created new families and unexpected problems. Some women who seemed submissive in their homeland became "Americanized," or independent, too quickly for their husbands. Many couples lived happily, but not all. Some Chinese American men, who imported brides from Hong Kong, found their wives behaved differently from their idealized recollection of traditional Chinese women. One new bride told her husband to find a better home in a week "or I get a divorce."

In Tokyo, Japan, in 1948 a U.S. soldier marries a Japanese woman. Many war brides entered the United States in the late 1940s.

President Harry Truman called for admission of 40,000 displaced persons (DPs) in Europe to be admitted outside of the quotas. In 1948 Congress passed a DP law that Truman signed though he called it "flagrantly discriminatory" against Catholics and Jews.

However, by this time, the government's definition of a DP was being altered to fit its cold war anticommunist policy. The overwhelming majority of immigrants to the United States after 1947 were victims not of Nazism but of communism, and they were admitted as "nonquota immigrants," a special status.

As "nonquota immigrants" thousands of people reached these shores from Latvia, Lithuania, and Estonia. Liberated from Nazi Germany by Stalin's Red army, these countries were taken over by puppet governments imposed by Moscow.

In DP camps refugees from Latvia, Lithuania, and Estonia began a Baltic university taught by college professors, farmers' committees, and the Foresters Association. These immigrants came to the United States along with their traditions, social groups, and religious and educational institutions, and newspapers.

By the time the DP law was extended in 1950 and again in 1956, it had become a key weapon in the battle against communism. Hundreds of thousands of people were taken in simply because they fled Communist governments in Poland, Hungary, Yugoslavia, China, and Indonesia. Federal officials recruited many of these people for their global conflict against Soviet Russia.

In 1950 Congress passed the Internal Security Act, and this made anticommunism American's commanding policy. The new law strictly prohibited entry by any person who favored communism. The law also permitted the deportation of any alien who was a Communist or became one after landing or becoming a citizen.

Then, in 1952, Congress passed the 300-page McCarran-Walter Act written by two leading Democratic Party followers of McCarthyism, Senator Pat McCarran and Representative Fred Walter. Their law admitted as anticommunist refugees even those who had supported the Nazi Party and carried out its programs of murder and genocide. However, the law excluded as immigrants those who fled dictatorships when the dictators claimed to be allied with the United States against communism.

McCarran and Walter did not disturb the quota system of the early laws because they wanted to ensure that 85 percent of the arrivals would be white people from Western Europe. To reduce the number of people of color to be admitted from the West Indies, the act set new, lower quotas for colonial areas. To further cut down on "undesirables," American foreign consuls were given new and arbitrary powers to evaluate and rule on the political and economic views of those who wanted to immigrate. President Truman vetoed the law with these words:

> The idea behind this discriminatory policy was, to put it boldly, that Americans with English or Irish names were better people and better citizens than Americans with Italian or Greek or Polish names…. Such a concept is utterly unworthy of our traditions and our ideals.

But at the height of McCarthyism, large majorities in the House and Senate passed the law over the President's veto. Presidents Eisenhower and Kennedy also denounced the law's discriminatory provisions, but the quota system was in effect between 1921 and 1965. By then, the foreign-born population in the United States had dwindled to only five percent of the American people.

Cold war anticommunism also welcomed a new kind of immigrant along with the thousands of displaced persons. The

Many displaced persons, such as these Europeans, sought homes in the U.S. after World War II.

Bernard Baruch, Advisor to Presidents

Bernard Baruch was born in 1870 to a Jewish immigrant family in South Carolina. By the time he was 30, he had become a rich man through wise investments.

Baruch became an advisor to American presidents from Woodrow Wilson to Lyndon Johnson. Wilson appointed Baruch to manage the Federal War Industries Board during World War I.

Baruch was trusted by conservative bankers and corporate heads to promote their views in government circles. During World War II, Baruch served as advisor to Secretary of State James Byrnes. President Franklin Roosevelt often vacationed at Baruch's South Carolina home.

After the war, Baruch wrote the government report detailing the country's conversion from wartime to peaceful economic growth. He represented America on the UN's Commission on Atomic Energy where he formulated the "open skies" plan to inspect nuclear sites by air. He was the first official to use the phrase "cold war" to describe the struggle against world communism.

Each president sought his advice. Baruch was always ready to share his wisdom with those who shaped the country he loved. ■

Wernher von Braun holding a model of the V-2 rocket he designed.

government, with the secret approval of Presidents Truman and Eisenhower and their secretaries of state, brought in 10,000 Nazis, including war criminals. This began in 1946 with "Operation Paper Clip" that brought Nazi scientists, such as Wernher von Braun, to work on rockets and nuclear delivery systems. Others, such as Klaus Barbie, the "Butcher of Lyons," France, came to the United States as cold war anticommunist experts. Barbie was subsequently allowed to live his life peacefully in South America until he was seized by Nazi hunters and returned to France for trial.

Former Nazis were often hired by the federal government as experts on Russia or communism. The CIA furnished them new identities, high-paying government jobs, and homes on tree-lined suburban streets. During the Red hysteria, many former Nazis joined American ethnic organizations and tried to guide them toward an anticommunism they had learned under Hitler. These immigrants paraded as anticommunist patriots. Since they had new identities, it was difficult to trace their views or to root them out of the ethnic groups they joined.

CHAPTER 9

RACE IN MID-CENTURY AMERICA

Barriers of law and custom often rigidly separated Americans in the 1950s. The Supreme Court had ruled in 1896 that separation by race was constitutional, and this remained the law of the land. In 30 states men and women of different races could not legally marry. The state constitutions of North Carolina, South Carolina, Florida, Alabama, Tennessee, and Mississippi forbade state legislatures to permit intermarriage.

States such as Arizona, California, Colorado, Indiana, Idaho, Montana, Nebraska, Oregon, North and South Dakota, Utah, and Wyoming also forbade intermarriage. Though the ban was aimed at African Americans, 15 states also specifically mentioned Asians or Native Americans.

Almost half of the 48 states required legal separation of races from nursery school thorough graduate school. State funds spent on white education were more than double that spent on people of color. Many of the best colleges had quota systems to limit the number of people of color and of Jewish Americans they admitted.

Three states mandated a triple segregation in public schools, to ensure that Native Americans, African Americans, and whites did not attend school together. Textbooks kept in storage in Florida and North Carolina were segregated according to the race of the pupils who used them.

The leading publishers issued books that did not offend white Southerners or created special texts designed to please them. Black people rarely appeared in textbooks except as contented slaves. Slavery was pictured as a kind and beneficial system.

Racist hiring practices were common in America. In 1948 a survey by the Anti-Defamation League found that state licensing

This NAACP booklet showed how Atlanta schools did not offer equal education to all.

boards were among the leading perpetuators of job discrimination. Application blanks were specifically designed to filter out people of color, Jews, and others considered undesirable. The survey found that 95 percent of the time the forms "ask questions which have no relation to competence in the fields of medicine, dentistry, law, optometry, and accounting."

In the South, segregation was a fixed way of life. Signs in stores, factories, public facilities, and buses told where "white" and "colored" could sit or stand. Lawmen had the power to arrest violators. In 1947 a black male passenger on a train entering North Carolina was awakened and told to move to the segregated car. When he refused, he was shot and killed by the conductor. A white jury acquitted the conductor, saying he had acted in self-defense.

Legal segregation could vary from one state to another. In the South, African Americans could buy a cup of coffee but could not sit down and drink alongside whites. Arkansas required separate voting booths for Blacks, and Georgia required separate Bibles for black witnesses in court. In South Carolina whites and Blacks could not work in the same factory room, line up at the same pay window, or use the same toilets, stairways, entrances, or exits. In Washington, D.C., a dog cemetery segregated the dead dogs belonging to African Americans from those owned by whites.

Voting rights were severely restricted in many states. A hundred thousand Native Americans could not vote in Arizona and New Mexico, and only a handful could vote in southern states.

Efforts to deny African Americans democratic rights also kept many white people from enjoying their rights. A poll tax in southern states, designed to keep elections "lily-white," also kept millions

Black war veterans in 1946 plan to register and vote in the South.

of poor white men and women from voting. This resulted in many southern senators and representatives being elected by five or ten percent of possible voters in their district.

Southern voter registration procedures made a mockery of democracy. Registrars eliminated any black voter who could not "understand" any part of the Constitution or explain complicated legal terms. In Mississippi, people could be denied the vote unless they said they opposed the Fair Employment

46

Practices Law, antilynching laws, ending poll taxes, and that they "cherish the customs and the time-honored [racial] traditions of the Old South." A black college professor was denied the right to vote because he could not read Chinese.

Perhaps nowhere was the lack of democracy more obvious and discrimination more glaring than in Washington, D.C. The nation's capital had a large African American citizenry and was run by a committee of Congress dominated by white Southerners. Residents were denied the vote and any management role. Within a few blocks of the White House, African Americans living in poverty were denied admission to white schools, stores, restaurants, recreational facilities, and institutions. Facilities for federal employees were segregated, and job benefits and advancement procedures largely benefited whites. Dr. Ralph Bunche, who received the Nobel Peace Prize in 1950, could attend a Washington theater only if he used the phone to order tickets and hid his race by asking for tickets with a French accent.

In the North, people of color did not face "colored" signs, but they still found they were denied access to public facilities, bars, and hotels. People of color in northern cities were rarely picked for juries and were granted only token representation among such civil service positions as police, firemen, and teachers.

In 1950 Dr. Ralph Bunche (left) won the Nobel Peace Prize for his work for peace in the Middle East.

Blacks found that moving into "white" neighborhoods exposed their families to danger. Black ghettoes were seedbeds for disease, early death, and despair. In January 1948, *Architectural Forum* surveyed a block in Harlem, New York City, and concluded: "At a comparable rate of concentration the entire United States could be housed in half of New York City." Harlem's leading stores were owned by whites who charged higher prices than stores in white areas and preferred to hire fellow whites as clerks.

The northern legal system was stacked against people of color. Local police acted like an army of occupation in ghetto neighborhoods and were often accused of using excessive force. The black 10 percent of the population accounted for half of all state executions in the United States. Along with Mexican Americans, Puerto Ricans, and other people of color, they were far more likely to be arrested, jailed, or executed than whites accused of the same crimes.

In 1949 many Native Americans lived in rural poverty near Carson City, Nevada, unable to find work or support families.

Discrimination assigned people of color to the lowest rung of the economic ladder and kept them there. In 1950, two-thirds of African American families had incomes of less than $3,000 a year, while only a fourth of whites were at this level. Mexican Americans and Puerto Ricans in eastern states had to live on incomes that were less than half of what white workers received.

Poverty stalked Native American reservations. Indian health standards were the lowest, their schooling the worst, and their death rate the highest in the country. The average Indian earned seven times less than whites. In the Navajo nation illiterates outnumbered those who could read by eight to one. Only one in four Native American children attended school, and their teachers were paid an average of $1,700 a year, half the national average.

Native Americans still encountered white hostility. Arizona and New Mexico interpreted their state constitutions to deny Indians voting rights. Native Americans sued in court, and in 1948 this discrimination finally ended.

Indian nations continued to break tradition to make progress. In 1951 Annie Dodge Wauneka became the first woman elected to the 74-member Navajo Council. She was a tireless fighter for her people and became the first Indian woman to receive the Presidential Medal of Freedom. Her words to her people were:

Annie Dodge Wauneka

> Send your children to school. Learn the new ways. What is good for the white man's children is good for ours. Prejudice and tradition must be overcome.

In 1953 federal policies of the 1930s designed to foster independence for Native Americans were reversed by the new administration of President Dwight D. Eisenhower. Congress urged ending federal aid programs for Native American nations and treating each member as an individual. Though this sounded progressive and democratic, it thrust a people not used to capitalistic ways into a legal situation organized by their enemies. Without the consent of Native American nations, Congress took authority for civil and criminal legal matters from Indian reservation leaders and handed it to the states.

The first Eisenhower administration effort touched the Menominees in Wisconsin, a wealthy nation that ran a profitable commercial forest. Withdrawal of federal aid led to economic disaster. The Menominee assets had to be used to pay taxes for services the federal government once provided. The Menominees had to learn Wisconsin's laws and how to apply them. In three years a Menominee hospital, a power plant, and lands had to be sold. The nation suddenly had no doctor, no high school, and little hope.

In January 1958, Lumbee Indians in Robeson County, North Carolina, dramatically asserted their rights though this meant fighting the Ku Klux Klan and a system that divided the races into three different school districts. Klansmen called a rally to frighten the Lumbees into accepting a 70-mile-a-day bus trip for their schoolchildren. When Klansmen lit a cross and began to make speeches, a thousand armed Lumbees charged and destroyed the Klan speaker system and electric generator, and terrified Klansmen fled.

School Texts and Race

Hostility toward America's various ethnic and racial groups was conveyed to millions of children through their textbooks. In 1949 the American Council on Education (ACE) examined American texts and found that Native Americans were portrayed as either "cruel, bloodthirsty" people or "noble redskins." "The cultural characteristics of Indian life, past or present," ACE noted, did not appear in schoolbooks.

Other ethnic groups fared worse. "Asiatic minorities... were frequently treated in a manner implying they were racially inferior." Except for "offensive generalizations," their role in building the country was ignored.

Hispanics, ACE noted, were scorned:

> The Spanish-speaking peoples of the United States were generally ignored; if not, they were sometimes dealt with in terms likely to intensify prevalent stereotypes.

African Americans, ACE found, were portrayed as "a childlike, inferior group of people." Pictures of African Americans in texts were even more offensive.

In 1960 the Anti-Defamation League examined school texts again. Referring to the ACE report, they found "those same criticisms... continued to be valid." ∎

C H A P T E R   10

Progress for Minorities

America's different ethnic identities began to recede during the Great Depression and World War II. This assimilation into the American melting pot continued and accelerated during the cold war. During the war and the Red Scare, many Americans felt safer if they did not display their foreign origins.

At the same time state legislatures began to eliminate the last vestiges of discrimination based on a person's national origins. In 1952 a California court declared unconstitutional its 1913 Alien Land Law that had discriminated against Asian Americans. By 1960, Jewish Americans reported a sharp drop in anti-Semitism.

Cold war refugees were encouraged to take the lead in the fight against global communism. In September 1954, the Assembly of Captive European Nations was established to bring about self-determination for nine countries — Albania, Bulgaria, Lithuania, Poland, Estonia, Czechoslovakia, Hungary, Latvia, and Romania. This and other anticommunist groups lobbied extensively in Washington for the liberation of their homelands.

Thousands of Russians, Ukrainians, and Poles arrived in the United States during the cold war years and began to publish religious and anticommunist papers. A migration from the Ukraine brought 85,000 people, including many professionals. Once here they formed choruses, art clubs, youth associations, symphony orchestras, economic journals, newspapers, and sports clubs.

Poles who fled Communist domination added new votes to Polish American communities. In 1949 Joseph Mruk was elected mayor of Buffalo, becoming the first Polish American to run a major city. By 1952, Republicans attempted to entice Polish American voters from the Democrats with promises to rid Poland of communism. In 1954 Edmund Muskie, whose father arrived at Ellis Island in

1903, was elected governor of Maine, the first Polish American to achieve this high office. By 1960, Muskie sat in the United States Senate, and 12 Polish Americans had seats in the House.

In 1948, following the Communist coup in their homeland, many Czechoslovakian men and women teachers and professionals fled to the United States. Czech American women soon formed a National Council of Women in Exile and used their Chicago headquarters to fight Nazism and communism.

Some 37,000 Lithuanian refugees, including many intellectuals, arrived during the cold war. They formed professional and literary societies, ran newspapers, and organized cultural festivals. Some took part in scientific, philosophical, religious, and educational work in the Lithuanian language. Others formed historical societies, opera companies, and women's clubs.

Maine governor Edmund Muskie in 1954

Latvians also fled their homeland in the wake of the Red army takeover, including 600 who settled in Wisconsin. Some started their own newspapers, Boy Scout troops, Lutheran and Catholic congregations, concerts, festivals, and protest groups. In 1950, 25 books written in the Latvian language had been published.

About 13,000 Hungarians entered the United States after 1948, many of them professionals and college students. Some formed their own Boy Scout troops. In 1956 these Americans organized rallies and relief activities in support of the 1956 revolt against Soviet troops in Hungary.

Greek Americans were proud that their country had defeated Mussolini and held off Nazi armies before they were overrun in World War II. When Greece was torn by internal warfare after World War II, the Truman Doctrine allowed American military intervention to prevent any government friendly to communism from coming to power. Though the McCarran Act had set a Greek quota of 308 people, an additional two to three thousand anticommunist Greeks were admitted as nonquota refugees.

Indiana congressman John Brademas

In 1959 John Brademas, the son of a Greek immigrant, was elected to Congress. A Democrat, he became a leading voice for public education in the United States. He left the Congress to serve for many years as president of New York University, the largest private college in the United States.

Chinese Americans were experiencing a new acceptance in the

Hiram Fong

United States that began with China's resistance to Japanese aggression in World War II. In 1946 when Wing F. Ong was elected to the Arizona legislature, he became the first Chinese American elected to a state legislature. In 1948 Hiram Fong was elected to the Hawaii legislature and became its speaker, and Ong was reelected in Arizona.

Then as Communist armies gained power over China, more than 1,100 Chinese anticommunists were admitted by Congress, about a thousand beyond their 105 quota. This was increased to 2,500 in 1949 as Chiang Kai-shek moved his government and troops to Formosa. Another 27,502 arrived in eight years under the McCarran Act. The ratio of women to men during this time became almost balanced. As U.S. hostility to Red China grew in the 1950s, many Chinese Americans became American citizens.

Chinese Americans also continued to rise in political life. In 1959 Delbert Wong was appointed a Los Angeles judge. That same year Hawaii became a state and elected Hiram Fong as the first Chinese American to sit in the U.S. Senate. One of 11 children born to sugar plantation laborers, Fong began picking beans when he was four. He put himself through the University of Hawaii and Harvard Law School with cash he earned shining shoes, selling papers, and working as a golf caddie. In 1957, the Nobel Prize in physics was awarded to two Chinese Americans, Princeton's Chen-ning Yang and Columbia University's Tsung-dao Lee.

Of 95 foreign-language papers published in the United States in 1946, 14 were in Chinese. By 1960, there were 11 Chinese dailies out of 65 foreign language papers.

Filipino Americans became eligible for American citizenship in 1946, and by 1948, Perfecto Bandalan had served on a trial jury in San Francisco. In 1953, during the Korean War, Filipino American branches of the American Legion and the Veterans of Foreign Wars won a speedier citizenship process for war veterans.

Filipino Americans also found increasing acceptance in the United States. In 1957 Dr. Primitva Demandante, one of two Filipino American doctors, became president of the American Women's Association. In 1960 in Seattle, Washington, Santiago Beltran was the first of his people admitted to a city police force.

Though depicted as sinister in World War II movies, Japanese Americans began to advance after the war. In 1951 Hollywood released *Go for Broke*, a movie about the heroic record of the 442nd Regiment. In 1953 Takeshi Yoshihara became the first Japanese American graduated from the Naval Academy. In California John Aiso was appointed to judgeship in Los Angeles.

Other Japanese Americans were elected to political office particularly in Hawaii. In 1957 Patsy Mink was elected vice president of the Young Democrats of America, and in 1964 she became the first woman of Asian ancestry to be elected to Congress. In 1957 James Kanno was elected mayor of Fountain City, California. In 1959 war hero Daniel Inouye, still in his thirties, was elected as Hawaii's first *Nisei* in Congress and then to the Senate in 1962.

Tom Kitayama was elected mayor of Union City, California. Wilfred Tsukiyama became the first Chief Justice of Hawaii's Supreme Court.

Arab Americans watched the crisis over Palestine in 1948 without the political clout to change American policy which favored Israel. Instead, they expanded their club network from Los Angeles and San Francisco to Oakland, Las Vegas, San Diego, Portland, Phoenix, and Seattle. By 1952, a Federation of Islamic Associations had been formed to spread information about Islam. One immigrant, Salom Rizik, wrote *Syrian Yankee* that year to describe how liberty and opportunity in the United States helped his career. In 1955 Arab Americans were able to build a mosque in Toledo, Ohio. A new level of their acceptance came in 1959 when the *Toledo Blade* announced their sacred holiday of Ramadan on its front page. That same year Arab American Michael Damas was elected mayor of Cleveland, Ohio. By 1960, George Coury became the first Arab American to own a seat on the New York Stock Exchange.

Those ethnic groups that had been part of the "new immigration" were also climbing political ladders. When John Pastore was elected to the U.S. Senate in 1950, he held the highest post ever attained by an Italian American. In 1953 three Italian Americans ran for mayor of New York City, and another, Carmine De Sapio, was the boss of New York's powerful Tammany Hall. In 1956 Alberto Rosselini was elected governor of Washington, and Foster Furcolo was elected Massachusetts' governor. In 1958 Michael Di Salle was elected governor of Ohio, and in 1961 John Volpe became the governor of Massachusetts and was reelected in 1965.

In 1964 congresswoman-elect Patsy Mink was welcomed to the White House by President Johnson.

John Pastore receiving a medal in 1950 honoring him as the outstanding Italian American in New England.

The first Swedish American appointed to a presidential cabinet was Clinton Anderson, chosen in 1946 by Harry Truman. In 1948 Minnesota sent Hubert Humphrey, whose mother was born on a farm near Kristiansand, Norway, to the Senate. Humphrey had distinguished himself at the Democratic convention for his strong stand on civil rights. After an unsuccessful attempt to gain the Democratic presidential nomination in 1960, Humphrey returned to the Senate.

Jewish Americans also reached high elective and appointive offices. New York governor Herbert Lehman was elected to the U.S. Senate in 1949. In 1950 Anna Rosenberg became assistant secretary of defense under George Marshall, the highest appointive post held by a Jewish American. In 1954 Abe Ribicoff was elected governor of Connecticut.

Portuguese Americans also climbed political ladders. In 1953 four Portuguese Americans served in Hawaii's lower house. In 1956 Clarence Azevedo became the mayor of Sacramento. In 1958 August Taveira was made a judge of Massachusetts' Superior Court, and in 1959 Arthur Carrellas, the son of immigrants from the Azores, was appointed to the same court.

Armenian Americans also had been making steady progress, and in 1952 Pergrouhi Svajian became a UN consultant on women's education. In 1960 Armenian American Samuel Mardian, Jr., was elected mayor of Phoenix, Arizona.

Governor Herbert Lehman, Eleanor Roosevelt, and Mayor Fiorello La Guardia headed the liberal wing of the Democratic Party.

CHAPTER 11

THE PUERTO RICANS

World War II enhanced the Puerto Rican desire for self-government. In 1946 President Truman appointed Jesus Piñero as the first native Puerto Rican governor of the Caribbean island. The next year Truman signed a law that allowed Puerto Rico to elect its own governor, and in 1948 Luis Muñoz Marín became the island's first elected governor. Marín had begun his political career by advocating independence from the United States. His father, Luis Muñoz Rivera, a prominent statesman since Spain had ruled the island, had studied in the United States.

Regulations from Washington that granted representation but not independence to Puerto Rico further antagonized citizens who sought self-determination for the island. In October 1950, five armed *independenistas* attacked the governor's mansion. Uprisings in Puerto Rican towns left 27 dead, 90 wounded, and a thousand arrested, including many women.

On November 1, 1950 *Independenistas* also struck in Washington, D.C., when two Puerto Ricans tried unsuccessfully to assassinate President Truman and were taken into custody. In 1954 Lolita Lebron and three male Puerto Ricans who lived in New York City opened fire on Congress and wounded four members of the House. The attackers went to jail.

Meanwhile, in 1951, Congress agreed to let Puerto Ricans write their own constitution, and a three to one majority on the island approved it though one-third of voters abstained. A year later the constitution was passed by the voting population. Congress approved it after President Truman called the document "an inspiration to all who love freedom and hate tyranny." That July, Governor Muñoz Marín proclaimed the island a commonwealth.

Beginning in 1945, many Puerto Ricans also began to leave their island for the United States to seek a better life. Seven out of ten acres on the island were rated poor or medium in productivity, and population density was more than ten times that of the United States. Residents lived with high birth and death rates, disease, unemployment, and poverty. Schools on the island did not compare with state systems in the United States.

The Puerto Rican migration was unique in several ways. First it was mostly a movement of employed people seeking better jobs, not the unemployed. It was also a migration of families, not single men. In 1946, when direct air flights between the island and New York City were established, it became the first major migration accomplished by air. As U.S. citizens rather than immigrants, Puerto Ricans were not subject to quotas or other restrictions.

By 1947, so many people had arrived that Puerto Rico's labor commissioner established a New York office. From 1946 to 1960, about 50,000 Puerto Ricans arrived each year. In 1953 alone, 69,124 had reached the city.

Puerto Ricans settled largely in a part of East Harlem they called "El Barrio." Other "El Barrios," or neighborhoods, spread out to the Bronx, parts of upstate New York, and New Jersey.

In New York the newcomers soon formed self-help organizations. Intellectuals started the Puerto Rican Forum to promote their interests. In 1961 the Forum started ASPIRA to promote higher education for New York Puerto Ricans. Like other new arrivals from all over the world, Puerto Ricans had quickly learned that education was the first rung up the ladder to success in America.

In 1954 Park and Madison avenues in midtown New York City were shopping areas for the wealthy. Uptown on 104th Street, the two avenues were home and playground to poor Puerto Ricans.

Most Puerto Ricans in these early years of migration lived among family and friends, usually in conditions of poverty. Yet in mainland "El Barrios" the newcomers sometimes were able to grasp new opportunities for work, home, and security. Irma Alvarado grew up in the 1950s, and "somehow I got it into my head that being Puerto Rican was wrong." She married a Puerto Rican who

> introduced me to a culture I hadn't known. He took me to
> Latin dances where I met lots of young Puerto Ricans,
> most working and many in college. They were bright,
> exciting. I wished I'd had friends like that as I'd grown up.

She made sure her children learned Spanish. "It's so important to me that my kids feel a pride and dignity in their heritage."

As the first generation of Puerto Ricans worked hard in crowded barrios, a second generation began to appear. The number of Puerto Ricans living in the suburbs doubled in the next 20 years.

One boy of 11 who left Puerto Rico to live in the United States was Herman Badillo. He was born in Caguas in 1929. His father, who was a teacher, and his mother both died a few years later, and young Herman Badillo arrived to live with an aunt on the mainland.

He finally settled in New York City where he attended public schools. He worked as a dishwasher, a cook, and a pin boy in a bowling alley and remembered Christmases without presents.

Badillo attended City College of New York and graduated from law school in 1954. He worked as an attorney and accountant for seven years, met Senator John Kennedy and helped in his campaign for the presidency.

Herman Badillo

In 1962, after Badillo was appointed deputy real estate commissioner by New York mayor Robert Wagner, he tried to help poor African American and Puerto Rican people in slums find decent homes. In 1965 he was elected borough president of the Bronx and tried to aid the poor of the borough. He campaigned for Democratic candidates, played a leading role in his party, and marched with those who opposed the war in Vietnam. In 1970 he ran for Congress and won, becoming the first Puerto Rican elected to that high office.

Roberto Clemente was an outstanding African Puerto Rican athlete who made his name on the mainland. Born poor in Puerto Rico in 1934, Clemente remembered how during World War II his

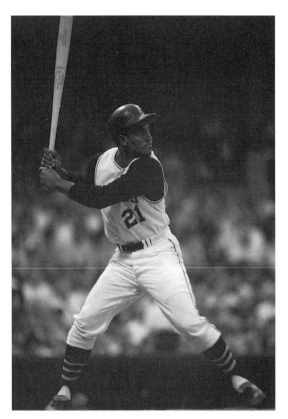

Roberto Clemente

parents "fed their children first and... took what was left. They always thought of us." A leading athlete in high school, he came to love baseball and turned down a chance to go to the 1952 Helsinki Olympic Games as a high jumper.

In 1953 a Brooklyn Dodger scout picked Clemente over 71 others. Early in his major league career, Clemente had a reputation for losing his temper which he later learned to control. When he joined the Pittsburgh Pirates in 1955, he quickly became a favorite of the fans, especially children. In 1960 the Pirates won the National League championship for the first time in 33 years. Clemente batted .314 during the season and .310 in the World Series with a hit in each game. The Pirates beat the Yankees in the final game.

In 1963 Clemente married Vera Cristina Zabala in Puerto Rico, and they bought a home near his parents on the island in Carolina. He won the National League batting title in 1965 at .329 and the next year was named the league's Most Valuable Player. In 1969 he hit three home runs in one game for the second time in his career. In 1970 more than 43,000 fans turned out for Roberto Clemente Night, and he recalled how emotional he felt knowing "so many are behind me." In the 1971 World Series Clemente was the star as the Pirates won the seventh game. The next year he got his 3,000th hit, a feat only ten baseball greats had accomplished.

Clemente donated thousands of dollars to charities and helped his poor or unfortunate friends. He began to build a Sports City in Puerto Rico hoping to help children avoid drugs. He died on New Year's Eve, 1972, when a plane he had filled with relief supplies for earthquake victims in Managua, Nicaragua, crashed at sea. In 1973 Clemente became the second diamond star in history to be voted into the Baseball Hall of Fame by special election.

The Mayor of San Juan

Felisa Rincón de Gautier, born in Ceiba, Puerto Rico, in 1897, was the oldest of seven children and helped raise her sisters and brothers after her mother died. Felisa and her family learned to love books, and their father often read to them after dinner. She also began to study her people's history.

Felisa left high school in her junior year, began to manage the family farm, *La Cermica*, and studied the hard life of the *jibaros*, or peasants. She and her family moved back to San Juan where she heard how American women were campaigning for the vote. In 1932 Puerto Rican women were granted suffrage, and Felisa defied her father's authority and registered as a voter. She joined the new Liberal Party and helped register voters in San Juan. After a stay in New York City in 1934 where she worked in the garment industry, she returned to Puerto Rico and opened "Felisa's Style Store."

The business was a success. But Felisa decided to become a key worker for Muñoz Marín and the Popular Democratic Party (PDP). In 1939 she married a fellow political worker, Jenar Gautier, an attorney and poet. The next year the PDP won a majority of votes in the Puerto Rican Senate, and Muñoz Marín was elected president of the Senate.

In 1945 Felisa took over the job of San Juan mayor when the incumbent left the position for another job. She quickly became known as a hardworking mayor who kept her office open to the public every Wednesday. Two years later, she was elected mayor on her own and then reelected three more times. Her husband, who had originally opposed her running for mayor, remained at her side as an assistant attorney general. Through unconventional methods, Felisa was able to help many poor people, though this often brought her criticism. She often led the New York City Puerto Rican Day parade and retired as mayor in 1968 at the age of 71. ■

CHAPTER 12

POSTWAR AFRICAN AMERICAN RESISTANCE

In 1946 President Truman heard some terrifying news. During the summer, as African American war veterans began to demand the democracy they had fought for, white southern mobs lynched six African American soldiers. In Monroe, Georgia, a veteran, his wife, and another black couple were pulled from a car, lined up, and shot. One body had 180 bullet wounds. That September Walter White of the NAACP described the lynchings to President Truman. "My God!" Truman said, "I had no idea it was as terrible as that."

Truman promised to do something. First the president issued Executive Order No. 9908 that created a presidential committee on civil rights. The next year Truman became the first president ever to address a convention of the NAACP. Later that year his commission's report, *To Secure These Rights*, called for a permanent Fair Employment Practices Commission, federal laws against lynching, and an unbiased system of justice. Truman also appointed the first African American, Judge William Hastie, governor of the Virgin Islands.

Judge William Hastie

However, African American people, even in southern states, were no longer waiting for officials to grant them rights. Thousands escaped from oppression by moving north. In 1920, 15 percent of African Americans lived in northern states; by 1940, the percentage reached 23 percent; in 1960, 40 percent; and by 1970, slightly more than 50 percent.

In northern cities African Americans could hold the balance of power in elections, and in certain large states they could hold the key in close national elections. Black political figures increasingly used this leverage to gain better jobs, housing, and education for urban African American communities.

A growing employer of African Americans was the Federal

Civil Service, where the number of people of color increased from 50,000 in 1933 to 200,000 in 1946. This and the teaching profession provided ladders into the middle class for African Americans.

Black voters and office seekers began to increase at the end of the war. In 1946, 30 African Americans, 18 Republicans, and 12 Democrats held seats in state legislatures.

The NAACP continued to hammer away at the walls of segregation after the war. In 1946 it took the case of Irene Morgan, who refused to move to the back of a Greyhound bus traveling between states. The Supreme Court declared that segregation was illegal in interstate commerce.

The National Negro Congress brought a petition for justice on behalf of African Americans to the United Nations Economic and Social Council. Though this brought no change in U.S. policy, it focused a world spotlight on the plight of African Americans.

In 1947 victories over racism increased. The Congress for Racial Equality (CORE) sent "freedom riders" into the South to test the enforcement of desegregation of interstate travel. NAACP attorney Thurgood Marshall pleaded for the right of African Americans to vote in the South Carolina Democratic primaries, and a white federal judge agreed. The CIO helped elect a black minister to the Salem, North Carolina, city council.

Meanwhile, segregation gradually ended in Washington, D.C. By 1947, black guests were accepted at the larger hotels and then at the theaters and movie houses. A. Philip Randolph formed the League for Non-Violent Civil Disobedience Against Military Segregation. He testified before Congress about his plans to organize a massive civil rights protest in 1948. President Truman issued Executive Order No. 9981 ending segregation in the U.S. armed forces.

In 1948, in a close presidential election with four candidates in the field, black agitation for equality increased. The Truman administration increasingly joined in legal challenges to segregation. After the attorney general joined in a suit, the Supreme Court declared that discriminatory housing covenants could not be enforced in

Blacks, including Walter White of the NAACP (left), picket the Stork Club in New York City because it did not serve African Americans in the 1940s.

A. Philip Randolph (right) testifying before Congress against discrimination in the U.S. armed forces in 1947.

state courts. The federal government began to enter cases in which black women successfully sued to enter southern law schools.

The election of 1948 proved to be a turning point for the country. Helped by African American voters, Harry Truman won a narrow victory over Republican Thomas Dewey. He also won out over two Democratic Party splinter groups — Dixiecrats who resented his stand for civil rights and Progressives who wanted to end the cold war and cooperate with the USSR.

The newly elected Truman administration prohibited racial discrimination in the civil service as it had in the armed forces. Many states in the Northeast passed fair employment laws. Southern border states began to admit one or two "token" black students to previously segregated white colleges. By 1949, Hollywood responded with four movies that spotlighted the problems caused by racial prejudice. In 1950 the Supreme Court ordered the admission of an African American student to the University of Texas, another to the University of Virginia, and another to Louisiana State University. Then the Supreme Court ruled that railroad dining cars could not refuse to serve people of color and outlawed a discriminatory Birmingham, Alabama, housing ordinance.

Despite these legal steps, the transition from segregation to integration was neither easy nor quick. In the armed forces black recruits were still barred from 198 of 460 job specialties and were allowed to enroll in only 21 of 106 courses for recruits.

However, the war in Korea, which began in June 1950, helped speed desegregation of the army. Two African Americans earned the Congressional Medal of Honor in that war.

When the NAACP sent Thurgood Marshall to Korea, he found that the army's "general practice is one of rigid segregation." Only two whites but 32 African American soldiers had been convicted of cowardice. Marshall said the 32 African Americans had withstood the ordeal of rigged trials.

The two strongest denunciations of the Korean War came from Paul Robeson and W.E.B. Du Bois. In the midst of the cold war, their calls for peace were made to appear subversive of U.S. interests, if not pro-Soviet.

When Dwight D. (Ike) Eisenhower was elected President in 1952, he carried only 21 percent of the black vote. African Americans recalled that then-General Eisenhower had testified in 1948 before Congress to oppose integration of the armed forces.

Two weeks after his election Ike met with an NAACP delegation and said he would not send federal funds to segregated districts. He also said he would not tell the South how to run its schools.

However, an NAACP case on behalf of five African American children was about to change American politics forever. In 1954 the Supreme Court unanimously agreed to tell school systems that segregation was no longer constitutional. In a unanimous vote in *Brown v. Topeka Board of Education*, the court called for desegregation of public schools "with all deliberate speed."

The NAACP case had been argued by its chief attorney, Thurgood Marshall, based on sociological and legal research that cost $100,000. Marshall was aided by a host of attorneys, including the NAACP's Jewish American lawyer, Jack Greenberg.

The public response to the *Brown* decision was mixed. Districts in eight states announced a partial desegregation of schools. President Eisenhower privately disagreed with the decision and never spoke in its favor. Southern senators later announced a campaign to reverse the decision, declaring it a violation of states' rights. Their statement did not rule out violence.

Within a month the first of hundreds of White Citizens' Councils (WCC) were formed in the southern states to fight desegregation by applying economic pressure to any who tried to promote it. The Ku Klux Klan promised a violent campaign to stop what it called a

Linda Brown's case became a landmark Supreme Court decision.

George E. C. Hayes, Thurgood Marshall, and James N. Nab celebrate the famous Brown *desegregation decision outside the Supreme Court in 1954.*

63

"Communist plot to destroy America." If it was unclear where America was headed, African Americans knew where they wanted to go and felt the Supreme Court had pointed the way.

Jackie Robinson

The biggest victory over racism in 1947 probably came when Jackie Robinson, an all-around athlete at the University of California, Los Angeles (UCLA), finally became a member of a major league baseball team. Born in 1919, Robinson grew up in California where he and his African American friends could only use the YMCA swimming pool on Tuesdays. At UCLA he starred in football, track, and baseball.

In World War II Robinson served as an officer and had been court-martialed for fighting discrimination. After the war, he played for the Kansas City Monarchs of the Negro American League. In 1945 he was scouted and then hired by Branch Rickey for the Brooklyn Dodgers but first sent to play for their farm team in Canada.

Robinson and Rickey had many talks that had nothing to do with hitting or fielding and a lot to do with handling white racism on the diamond. In his first season in the majors in 1947, the young second baseman dealt with racial insults from crowds, opposing teams, and his own teammates. In some cities he had to stay in a different hotel than the white Dodgers.

Though he had to swallow a lot of hatred on the field, Robinson's hitting, baserunning, and fielding made for a fine rookie year. In 1949 he was named the National League's Most Valuable Player. Robinson became one of the most exciting players the game had ever produced, and he led his team to six pennants and a World Series victory. By the time he retired in 1956, the color line in professional sports had been broken and the American pastime had been permanently desegregated. ■

Jackie Robinson begins a double play at second base.

CHAPTER 13

NONVIOLENT TEST IN MONTGOMERY

Revolutions are not sudden explosions but erupt from long-burning fires of misery. The civil rights crusade that began in 1955 had been building since the arrival of the first ships bringing Africans to the New World. Centuries of slave rebellions and other resistance preceded the Constitution and the Civil War. In the name of freedom African Americans in the Civil War and two world wars were handed rifles and sent into battle. But then returning veterans were asked to swallow white supremacy.

On Thursday, December 1, 1955, in Montgomery, Alabama, the first capital of the old Confederacy, something happened. Rosa Parks, a seamstress and a secretary of the local NAACP, left work and did some shopping. Then she boarded the bus for her regular ride home. Her ride was to be anything but regular.

Rosa Parks in her own quiet way began what has been called "the Second American Revolution."

The 36 seats soon filled up with 14 whites seated in the front and 22 African Americans seated in the back. When a white man entered, the bus driver, J.P. Blake, asked the four black people seated behind the last white row to give up their seats for whites. This was common procedure. But this time the four, including Rosa Parks, did not move. When Blake demanded they vacate the seats, three took different seats but not Rosa Parks. Blake said she was sitting in the white section, which was wherever he said it was, and told her she could be arrested.

Parks answered she was not moving, speaking so softly her voice ordinarily would not have been heard above the bus noises. But no one was talking, and everyone was listening. Later she recalled, "There was no plan at all. I was just tired from shopping."

Two policemen escorted Rosa Parks to the station where she was booked, fingerprinted, and put in a jail cell. Her mother called

E.D. Nixon, head of the local Brotherhood of Sleeping Car Porters and the state NAACP, and he called the police desk sergeant. When the sergeant refused to reveal the charges against Parks and hung up on him, Nixon knew a racial code had been defied. He called Clifford Durr, an attorney, and his wife, Virginia, who were white civil rights activists whose relatives included Supreme Court Justice Hugo Black. The Durrs rode by and picked up Nixon, and together they bailed Mrs. Parks out of jail. For the Durrs and Nixon, this was the case they had been waiting for to test segregation.

When Parks asked her husband if she should agree to be a test case, he answered, "The white folks will kill you, Rosa." But she finally decided to pursue the case because, as she said, "it will mean something to Montgomery and do some good."

One of the first groups contacted for support was the Local Women's Political Council at Dr. Martin Luther King, Jr.'s, Dexter Avenue Baptist Church. They met that night to develop a strategy and inform the community. Their leaflet called for a bus boycott.

> Until we do something to stop these arrests, they will
> continue. The next time it may be you, or you or you. This
> woman's case will come up Monday. We are, therefore,
> asking every Negro to stay off the buses on Monday in
> protest of the arrest and trial.

Nixon next spoke to Reverend David Abernathy and Dr. King. That evening at his church King hosted a meeting of 50 black leaders who agreed to organize a boycott. On Monday morning the plan exceeded everyone's expectations. The first three buses that passed the King residence had no riders. King then jumped into his car, drove around the city, and found that the buses had no or few black riders. Montgomery police commissioner Clyde Sellers told his police that only "goon squads" of black thugs could keep people off the buses and dispatched heavily armed police to follow them. They found no goon squads, but instead this police presence probably frightened away some Blacks who might have taken buses.

The next day Rosa Parks was convicted of violating a segregation ordinance and fined $14, but her lawyer announced she would appeal. Nixon walked out of the courtroom to post a bond so Parks could be released and found a crowd of 500 black men and women filling the court hallways out into the street. Even the lawmen with shotguns looked worried. When Nixon told the crowd he would bring out Parks right away, some shouted back that if the two did not appear in a few minutes, they would storm the courthouse and rescue them. It was a new day in Montgomery.

That evening black community leaders assembled to plan their campaign. King, at 26, recently married, and even more recently installed as pastor of the Dexter Avenue Church, was chosen president of what was later named the Montgomery Improvement Association (MIA). The choice was made not because of King's talents, which were unknown then, but because as the city's newest minister, he had the fewest enemies. King had only half an hour to jot down notes for his talk before a huge protest meeting.

In 1956 Dr. King and his wife Coretta hold their daughter Yolanda in Montgomery, Alabama.

King began the meeting by saying "first and foremost — we are American citizens — and we are determined to apply our citizenship — to the fullest of its means." He thanked Mrs. Parks for the "boundless outreach of her integrity… the height of her character… the depth of her Christian commitment." Then he said, "There comes a time when people get tired of being trampled over by the iron feet of oppression." Thousands cheered and applauded.

"If we are wrong," he said, then the Supreme Court and God Almighty, Jesus of Nazareth, "are also wrong." The audience again erupted into noise, and he had to pause to make his conclusion.

> And we are determined here in Montgomery — to work
> and fight until justice runs down like water, and
> righteousness like a mighty stream.

When Reverend Abernathy organized car pools that first night, 150 people volunteered their cars. This tactic supplied rides for half of the Blacks in Montgomery, but beginning that cold December, the other half walked to work for more than a year.

Montgomery's city government started to negotiate with the MIA. Then it broke off talks and leading officials publicly joined the White Citizens' Council (WCC). In the second month of the boycott, and while Dr. King was off making a speech, a bomb exploded on the porch of his home, but his wife and child were unhurt. King urged his followers never to retaliate with violence.

After 80 days of successful boycotting, the city administration ordered the arrest of Dr. King and 100 others it called leaders. The next night Dr. King told a mass meeting the boycott would continue no matter how many people went to jail. The conflict, he said, was not "between the white and the Negro" but "between justice and injustice." He called on his followers not to hate but to love those who opposed them as they pursued their nonviolent resistance to injustice.

Dr. King's theory of "nonviolent resistance" began to gain national attention as an effective way of challenging centuries of racial hatred and discrimination. The NAACP defended King and the other boycott figures, and a federal court finally overturned the Montgomery segregation ordinance. Another NAACP suit forced the Interstate Commerce Commission to outlaw segregated buses and waiting rooms. Two additional NAACP suits resulted in Supreme Court rulings that banned segregation in public recreation facilities.

The walls of segregation appeared to be falling rapidly in 1956, at least in the upper South, as 326 school districts desegregated. Among the states that had made progress toward integration were Oklahoma, Kansas, Missouri, Delaware, Maryland, West Virginia, and Texas. The NAACP, however, filed 33 desegregation suits in the Deep South, to no avail. States in the Deep South refused to even consider "token" integration.

Meanwhile, the Klan became active again, and lynching reappeared in the South. When Reverend George Lee and Gus Courts led a drive that registered 400 Blacks to vote in Humphreys County, Mississippi, Lee was lynched. An assassination attempt was made on Courts. Then White Citizens' Councils brought economic and other pressure on the newly registered voters, and most withdrew their names from the rolls.

In Congress, meanwhile, Adam Clayton Powell, Jr., Emmanuel Celler, and Senator Herbert Lehman tried to aid desegregation. Some 100 bills were offered, but none passed. Powell kept introducing bills to deny federal funds to segregated districts and segregated federal housing projects, and to desegregate state National Guard units, but with no success. NAACP pressure led to the passing of desegregation bills in New York and New Jersey.

As the Montgomery boycott headed toward its second Christmas of walking to work, 101 southern congressmen issued an appeal for massive resistance to the *Brown* decision of 1954. They blamed "outside agitators" and federal intervention in southern affairs. White Citizens' Councils now claimed more than 300,000 members and took part in drives to eliminate registered black voters from the voting rolls and to endorse racist candidates.

Finally, the Montgomery Bus Company, facing bankruptcy, agreed to hire African Americans as drivers, end racial segregation, and courteously accept all who took the bus. On the early morning of December 21, 1956, Dr. King and the Reverend Glenn Shirley, a white supporter of the boycott, boarded the bus near King's home. "We are glad to have you," the driver said in greeting them.

But all was not peaceful that year. A shotgun blast was fired into the King home two days before Christmas but injured no one. On Christmas Eve, a bomb exploded under the bed of boycott leader Reverend Fred Shuttlesworth, but he escaped unharmed.

The Montgomery boycott provided some important lessons. African Americans had discovered a mother lode of strength and unity. A black community in the Deep South had found it could unify across lines of sex, church affiliation, and class.

By adopting Dr. King's nonviolent resistance beliefs, African Americans had found a way to combat unjust laws and to affirm American ideals. Black people had found their church was a bastion and gathering point for armies of peaceful resisters. In Dr. King they had found a charismatic leader. Last but not least, the African American community found some allies in the white community willing to make sacrifices for equal justice.

Martin Luther King in 1956 tells his cheering followers that the bus boycott would continue until victory was won.

From the outset in the battle for civil rights, women had marched in the front ranks. As more families had moved into urban areas, women's expectations had risen and intensified a thirst for their own rights. Black women who had tasted opportunity during the war were hardly willing to return to demeaning work serving whites. Their devotion inspired a movement and provided it with important leaders such as Rosa Parks.

King and the other leaders in Montgomery knew that even more important battles lay ahead. They hoped the victory in Montgomery would lead to a spiritual awakening of their people and perhaps all Americans. In February 1957, King became president of the Southern Christian Leadership Conference (SCLC) and with 60 preachers sought to coordinate efforts at school desegregation, voter registration, and broad attacks on the entire legal and social system that limited African Americans.

There was no turning back now. "We want the right to vote now," King had announced to kick off the SCLC voter registration campaign. "We do not want freedom fed to us in teaspoons over another 150 years." To serve as acting executive director of SCLC headquarters in Atlanta, King picked the dynamic organizer, Ella Baker, who had successfully recruited NAACP youth groups throughout the South. Nevertheless, he was concerned whether a woman could manage the job and whether the other ministers would respect her. Baker also had doubts about the ministers' ability to respect her, but she knew that was their problem. She plunged into her work without a phone or a mimeograph machine but within months had voter registration projects rolling ahead in a dozen cities. In a year she claimed active voter registration operations in ten southern states. And she had just gotten started.

The Emergence of Martin Luther King, Jr.

Martin Luther King, Jr., was born in 1929 to a minister's family in Atlanta. At 15 he entered Moorehouse College, then went on to Crozer Theological Seminary where he began to study the philosophy of nonviolence preached by Mohandas Gandhi to free India from British colonial rule. King began to wonder if this idea had some application to the struggle of his own people to achieve first-class citizenship in America.

King was ordained a minister in 1947. He attended Boston University where he received a doctorate and met Coretta Scott, a talented singer training for a concert career. In 1953 the couple married and settled down in Atlanta. The next year King became minister of the Dexter Avenue Baptist Church in Montgomery, AL, and in December 1955 he was chosen to lead the Montgomery boycott. King's house was bombed, shotgunned, and he was arrested, but he would not be intimidated.

King formed the Southern Christian Leadership Conference to promote other nonviolent actions to win civil rights. He and the SCLC supported the Freedom Riders, the sit-ins, and many other drives for equal justice. These culminated in the historic March on Washington in 1963. ■

CHAPTER 14

DESEGREGATING THE
SCHOOLS

In the year after the Supreme Court ordered integration of the nation's educational system in 1954, some 500 school districts in the upper South had desegregated. Black and white children sat side by side in Baltimore and Washington, D.C., and schools in Virginia had begun to open their doors not on the basis of race but by neighborhood. Everywhere children and parents of both races accepted the change more easily than anyone predicted. Only where there was organized opposition by fanatical segregationists did trouble erupt.

Public education had been the means of achievement for the nation's immigrants, and now it had been ordered to serve children of color on an equal basis. In Hoxie, Tennessee, 26 African American children enrolled in a white system of 800 students. Then a few white parents tried to frighten the community with fears of interracial marriages. Anxious parents asked the Hoxie Board of Education to halt school integration, but the board held firm, and the issue died.

The Deep South's leading officials were defiant, committed segregationists. They took no steps toward desegregation until they faced court orders. In Georgia, Governor Herman Talmadge proclaimed that his state "would not tolerate the mixing of the races in the public schools" or anywhere else.

Even where courts ordered desegregation, the process could be painful. Autherine Lucy was admitted to the University of Alabama under a federal court order, but she was greeted by rioting white students. The college then removed her "for her own safety." President Eisenhower said he wished the various parties could settle the matter peacefully and did nothing. Lucy then sued to enter the university, but it expelled her knowing the federal government would not act. It took seven more years before the University of Alabama opened its doors to students of all races.

In 1956 neither major political party endorsed the *Brown* decision. President Eisenhower and Democratic candidate Adlai Stevenson said they thought it would be wrong and useless to use troops to enforce court decisions. Eisenhower said that one could not legislate against hatred. In 1956 only 200 school districts desegregated their schools, and in 1957 the figure was only 38.

The President had hoped the common sense of the American people would bring about compliance with the law. But as the new school term began in 1957, Eisenhower found common sense has its limitations. Governor Orval Faubus of Arkansas disobeyed a court order to admit nine qualified African American youths to Central High School in Little Rock. On the radio he announced there would be bloodshed if the nine entered the school, and he called out the National Guard to protect Central High.

The governor's inflammatory announcements brought a menacing crowd of segregationists to the front of the school. The black children had been warned not to attend and stayed home, but Elizabeth Eckford, 15, had not heard that the National Guard would prevent her entering Central High School. Eckford walked toward the school. Guardsmen, she recalled, "raised their bayonets," and she had to turn around and head home. A jeering crowd followed her, some yelling "Lynch her," as she walked to the bus stop. A white reporter from the North put his arm around her, and a white women from Arkansas put her on the bus.

The world news media carried the story of Elizabeth Eckford's bravery and of Governor Faubus's defiance. President Eisenhower reluctantly ordered the 101st Airborne Division to move into Little Rock to enforce the court ruling invoking his presidential powers to "federalize" the Arkansas National Guard and place it under his control.

Federal paratroops guarded the entrances and the corridors of Central High School. They brought the nine youths to school each day in armed convoys and also sped them home each night.

Inside the school, teachers tried to help everyone adjust, and some white children made offers of friendship to the newcomers. Outside the school, segregationists gathered daily to show their hatred of the federal government, the troops, the court order, and Blacks. When some white students called for a walkout to protest

U.S. Army troops escort black students to Central High School in Little Rock, Arkansas.

the presence of the nine black students, fewer than 60 of the 1,800 students joined them.

The troublemakers within the school began to focus on one of the nine, Minnejean Brown, 16. They cursed at, tripped, or pushed her at every opportunity. After five months, Brown lost her patience and struck back when someone in the school cafeteria spilled hot soup on her. The principal suspended both pupils. Brown left for New York where she entered the private New Lincoln School and graduated a year later with high honors. Ernest Green, who graduated in 1958 from Little Rock's Central High with 600 white students, went on to become an assistant secretary in the U.S. Department of Labor.

Governor Faubus soon became the loudest voice for segregation in the country. He finally closed all three Little Rock high schools for the 1958-1959 term. But a federal court found the closing unconstitutional, and the Board of Education forced the schools to reopen. This time three African American children, including Elizabeth Eckford, went to school, and local police kept order.

Meanwhile, a new nonviolent assault was being launched on segregation. In 1958 African American students in Kansas and Oklahoma began "sit-in" demonstrations at lunch counters in which they demanded the right to be served. If they were not served, they refused to leave until they had been waited on.

The "sit-in" movement gathered real force in Greensboro, North Carolina, on February 1, 1960, when four black college students sat on stools in a five-and-ten-cent store and refused to move unless they were served coffee. The manager turned to a reporter and said, "They can just sit there. It's nothing to me." The students continued to sit and returned the next day to sit some more. By the fourth day, white students had joined them. After several months of sit-ins, the lunch counter was integrated.

A Mississippi college student in 1963 is dragged from a lunch counter and beaten by white segregationists.

Less than three weeks later, black students at Alabama State College in Montgomery staged the first sit-in demonstration in the Deep South. Two days later in Nashville 100 students were arrested during their sit-in. Then sit-ins led by high school or college students began to spread to hundreds of other southern cities. When white segregationists sometimes poured coffee, sugar, or milk over the demonstrators, some sit-ins erupted into riots. In the first six months of the movement over 1,600 young men and women, black and white, were arrested. By the end of 1961, sit-in demonstrators had convinced Woolworth and other chain stores in 114 cities to serve all their customers equally.

This dramatic change can largely be credited to the formation, in April 1960, of the Student Nonviolent Coordinating Committee (SNCC). Ella Baker played a key role in this conference and the formation of the SNCC, which sought to unify efforts of students and young people to speed the pace of desegregation.

The nonviolent protest movement grew. In August, white church services in Atlanta were the target of "kneel-ins" by African American students and parents. Black leaders had begun to call Sunday morning at church the most segregated time in America.

In 1957 the first civil rights legislation in 82 years passed Congress largely through the efforts of Senate majority leader Lyndon Johnson of Texas. Johnson's effort made him a national political figure for the first time. The new law allowed Justice Department attorneys to sue in court for African Americans who had been denied voting rights. The law also established a Civil Rights Commission to investigate and make recommendations for new legislation.

In 1960 Congress and the President agreed to strengthen the 1957 law. This time the new bill was guided through Congress by two Democratic senators who had their eye on the White House, John F. Kennedy and Lyndon B. Johnson. The 1957 and 1960 laws did little more than declare that the federal government would no longer sit idly by as states denied citizenship rights to people of color. But this was a new and significant announcement. Previous administrations had accepted the white southern political argument that "states' rights" denied federal officials any power to protect African American rights in the states.

C H A P T E R 15

THE ELECTION OF KENNEDY

In the summer of 1960 the big political news was the Democratic Party's nomination of John F. Kennedy as their presidential candidate on the first ballot. An Irish American and a Catholic, Kennedy picked Lyndon Johnson as his running mate. The Republicans picked the incumbent vice president, Richard Nixon.

Kennedy's Catholicism reminded voters of Al Smith's defeat in 1928. Furthermore, a Catholic in the White House posed serious problems for many if not most voters. Before the summer was over, Kennedy decided to tackle the issue head-on. He appeared before the Ministerial Association in Houston, Texas, and told this gathering of Protestant clergymen that he firmly believed in separation of church and state and that if he could not solve a conflict between his duty as president and his religion, he would resign the presidency. His speech was warmly applauded.

In a series of televised debates with Nixon, Kennedy appeared to shine. Millions whose parents or grandparents had been born abroad saw in Kennedy a validation of their American quest. The senator found support in urban ethnic communities that usually had backed Democrats and carried many city districts in the election.

The African American vote, which in six of the eight most populous states

Senator John F. Kennedy campaigns in 1960.

75

held the balance of power in close elections, was vital to Kennedy's campaign. Also, more than a million African American men and women now were registered to vote in southern states. Both major parties took strong stands for civil rights.

In late October, Dr. Martin Luther King, Jr., was sentenced to four months of hard labor in Atlanta for taking part in a sit-in at a restaurant. The Nixon campaign said nothing. But Kennedy called Mrs. Coretta Scott King to offer his help and then had his brother Robert phone the trial judge. The following day King was released on bail. When Mrs. King revealed the story to civil rights leaders, it quickly became front-page news.

On Election Day 68,832,818 voters went to the polls in the largest turnout in American history (11 percent more than 1956). In one of the closest elections, Kennedy's victory margin was just 112,881 votes, or two-tenths of one percent. Kennedy had carried the largest states, thanks largely to African Americans who voted Democrat by 70 percent, an increase of 30 percent over the previous election. Kennedy also held other ethnic constituencies in major cities. A switch of 5,000 Illinois votes and 28,000 Texas votes would have placed Nixon in the White House.

Henry Barbosa Gonzales

One of those Democrats who rode into power with Kennedy was Henry Barbosa Gonzales, the first Mexican American elected to Congress from Texas. Born in 1916 in San Antonio to descendants of 16th-century Basque landowners and silver-mine owners, he had been turned away from city swimming pools and restaurants. Gonzales taught himself to speak English, graduated from law school, and became an attorney. During World War II, he was a naval intelligence officer. He entered politics and by 1957, had become mayor *pro tempore* of San Antonio. He could not afford to bring his wife Bertha and their eight children from San Antonio when he was elected to Congress, so he rented a small apartment.

As of 1992, Gonzales has served in Congress for 32 years. He has a scrappy reputation, having fought many battles for human rights, often challenging White House stands and scolding presidents. The 1960 election also saw Armenian American Samuel Mardian, Jr., a Republican, elected as mayor of Phoenix, Arizona.

Kennedy's inauguration speech boldly challenged "a new generation" to take up the fight for liberty. He spoke at a time when ethnic minorities who proudly identified with the first Roman Catholic American president were fast losing their ethnic identity. Many children of immigrants had stopped speaking the old languages, and most of their children could not speak a foreign language at all.

African Americans were filled with hope. "What a wonderful President we have now," said Reverend Fred Shuttlesworth in Birmingham, Alabama. The Kennedy inaugural festivities were organized by singer Frank Sinatra and had an interracial cast that included Leonard Bernstein, Harry Belafonte, Jimmy Durante, Ella Fitzgerald, Mahalia Jackson, and Sidney Poitier. A week later, Sinatra arranged a fund-raiser for Dr. Martin Luther King, Jr., in New York that again assembled a multiethnic all-star cast.

The Kennedy years ushered in a great pride among ethnic minorities on the one hand but a lessening of their efforts to preserve their cultural heritage and an accelerated push to adapt to the new American civilization on the other hand. "I feel like a chicken that has hatched a duck's egg," said one immigrant about her offspring.

CHAPTER 16

THE "NEW FRONTIER" AND MINORITIES

John F. Kennedy, who in 1958 had written *A Nation of Immigrants* to celebrate the contributions of the 42 million people who came to these shores, was an inspiration to ethnic America. In July 1963, President Kennedy called on Congress to remove all discriminatory immigration quotas. He referred to this and other parts of his program for America as a "New Frontier."

The Kennedy administration's new Indian commissioner, Philleo Nash, tried to focus public attention on the plight of the 509,000 Native Americans, including 453,000 on reservations. Nash noted that Native Americans earned from a quarter to a third of what white Americans did, had four-and-a-half times the white unemployment rate, had half the education, and a life expectancy that was two-thirds of white Americans'. His focus was education, and he announced 963 scholarships for Indians in 1963 alone.

In 1960, 12 Polish Americans were elected to Congress, the largest number up until that time. In 1963 Kennedy appointed John Gronouski as postmaster general. Gronouski was the first Polish American to sit in a presidential cabinet.

In 1961 Italian American John Volpe was elected governor of Massachusetts and reelected four years later. In 1962 Kennedy appointed Anthony Celebrezze, a former mayor of Cleveland, his secretary of health, education, and welfare.

In the three years of the New Frontier, other ethnic minorities made progress. Arthur Goldberg, a Jewish American union attorney, became Kennedy's secretary of labor in 1961 and then was appointed to the United States Supreme Court.

The Filipino American residents of Seattle finally had one of their number, Santiago Beltran, on the city police force. In 1961 Chinese American students numbering 1,300 attended 88 American colleges. In 1962 Wing Luke, 36, was elected to the Seattle city council and became its temporary president.

In 1961 Arab American women became more politically active. They formed a society that studied Middle East issues, provided aid to young Palestinians, and examined American school texts for anti-Arab bias.

Senator Daniel Inouye

Japanese Americans continued their political advance. In 1962 Congressman Daniel Inouye of Hawaii was elected to the U.S. Senate, and Masayuki Matsunaga was elected to the House seat Inouye had vacated. In 1962 Seiji Horiuchi became the first *Nisei* elected to the Colorado legislature and the first Japanese American sent to a mainland legislature.

Korean Americans became increasingly concerned about the lack of democracy in Korea. In 1961 a team sent to tour Korea and survey conditions after student riots included Robert Chang of Hawaii's House of Representatives. In 1963 a former South Korean general and chief of staff, Choi Kyong-nok, led a march in front of the White House to protest his homeland's military government. In 1962 Alfred Song was elected to the California assembly.

In 1962 Portuguese American Joe Gonsalves left his position as mayor of Cerritos and was elected to the state assembly. He served for 12 years and became chair of the important Assembly Committee on Taxation and Revenue. Arab American Frank Maria was selected to serve on the U.S. delegation to UNESCO.

Fidel Castro's victory in Cuba in 1959 spurred a migration of Cubans to the United States. By 1962, more than 155,000 people sailed to the United States as refugees and were granted asylum as anticommunists. Many arrivals were educated and from the professional and business classes, people who resented Castro's imposition of a planned economy. Some 2 percent of arrivals were Chinese Cuban. Few African Cubans left the island since they felt Castro was truly responsive to their welfare.

Cuban refugees arriving in Miami, Florida, in 1961.

A federal Cuban Refugee Program welcomed newcomers and tried to settle them in places other than southern Florida where about 99 percent of the Cuban immigrants lived, straining the resources of schools, housing, and medical and welfare institutions. By 1964, more than 170,000 refugees had registered with the Cuban Refugee Center in Miami. Some 300,000 were sent to other parts of the country, and some chose Puerto Rico.

Cuban immigrants almost immediately formed a series of societies, some of which made plans to free their homeland from Castro. In this effort they were encouraged by both the Eisenhower and Kennedy administrations. Then, in 1961, came the disastrous Bay of Pigs invasion, planned by the CIA during the Eisenhower years and carried out under Kennedy. Kennedy had to ransom hundreds of captured Cuban refugees, but he promised them a free Cuba.

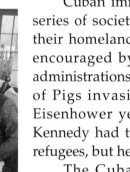

In October 1962 President Kennedy (right) meets with air force officers regarding the Cuban missile crisis.

The Cuban missile crisis the following year brought the United States and the USSR very close to nuclear war, but a solution was negotiated peacefully by the President and Soviet leader Nikita Khrushchev. This settlement and the humiliating American defeat at the Bay of Pigs solidified Castro's hold on the island. But this drove more refugees to the United States. Once again those who left were largely white and middle class. Puerto Rico replaced Cuba as an attractive Caribbean vacationland for Americans.

African Americans were also able to make political strides during the Kennedy years. In 1961 August Hawkins was elected to Congress from California and then reelected three more times. Harlem congressman Adam Clayton Powell, Jr., became the chairman of the important Education and Labor Committee. Robert Weaver became an administrator for the Federal Housing and Home Finance Agency, the highest position a Black ever held.

August Hawkins

President Kennedy appointed three prominent African Americans to judicial offices: NAACP attorney Thurgood Marshall to the Federal Court of Appeals; James B. Parson to a federal district court; and Marjorie Lawson to a local judgeship in Washington, D.C. Clifton Wharton, who had been a minister to Romania, became Kennedy's ambassador to Norway.

The civil rights movement dramatically emphasized how women could change society. From students to adult organizers, the courage of African American women inspired women the world over. Women not only participated in the campaign to elect Kennedy, but there was a steady rise in the number of women in Congress from 8 in 1948 to 17 in 1956 and 20 in 1961.

In 1962 young Cesar Chavez tried to unite Mexican American farm workers into a union in the Southwest. One of the first organizers he recruited was Jesse Lopez de la Cruz, 43, a woman who had been laboring in grape, apricot, beet, and cotton fields since her childhood.

Cesar Chavez

Chavez's choice acknowledged the new role some women had taken in unions, civil rights groups, and political campaigns. Esther Peterson, the Kennedy administration's director of the Women's Bureau of the Department of Labor, persuaded the President to appoint a Commission on the Status of Women. It was chaired by Eleanor Roosevelt, directed by Peterson, and composed of women from labor unions, women's organizations, and government agencies. The commission reported back that an Equal Rights Amendment to the Constitution was not needed "now." However, it stressed unfair burdens society placed on women — job discrimination, unequal pay, lack of child-care services, legal inequality, and lack of key opportunities.

President Kennedy ordered the civil service to hire for career positions solely on the basis of merit not sex. Congress passed the Equal Pay Act in 1963 that eliminated separate rates of pay for men and women. Also, within a year, most states had formed commissions on women and had begun to discuss women's status and how to solve problems of inequality.

That same year Betty Friedan published *The Feminine Mystique*, which charged that women had been forced from public life into private home tasks as mothers. She called this "the problem that has no name" and urged women to seek work outside the home. Friedan was flooded with hundreds of letters from housewives who thanked her for her daring book.

A new women's revolution was brewing. It grew out of the civil rights movement, the increased participation of women in politics, and a book that laid bare a problem without a name.

CHAPTER 17

KENNEDY AND CIVIL RIGHTS

The Kennedy administration inherited a civil rights crusade determined to march forward to victory. Conflict was inevitable. In 1960 five southern states maintained totally segregated school systems. Only one in a hundred southern black students sat in integrated classrooms.

In the North segregation was enforced not by law but by quiet agreement among white officials. Northern schools adopted "token" integration — the admission of one or a few people of color to white schools. When schools admitted more than a handful of African Americans, they were usually "tracked" into special classes that did not prepare them for college. "Tokenism" and "tracking" were used to undermine school desegregation.

The Kennedy White House knew that the thorny issue of civil rights could split a Democratic Party that was "home" for both southern segregationists and African American voters. The president and his staff hoped to avoid the issue.

However, a few months after his inauguration, Kennedy had no choice but to wrestle with human rights issues. A new spirit of defiance, largely stemming from young, educated African Americans, was expressed by the students of Barber-Scotia College in North Carolina:

> We want the world to know that we no longer accept the
> inferior position of second-class citizenship. We are
> willing to go to jail, be ridiculed, spat upon, and even
> suffer physical violence to obtain first-class citizenship.

In the spring of 1961 this spirit also powered the Congress of Racial Equality (CORE), a small civil rights group dedicated since World War II to fighting segregation through direct, nonviolent action. CORE director James Farmer rounded up six black males, three white females, and three white males to take "Freedom Rides" into the South to test court-ordered desegregation of buses and terminals. John Lewis and another black student were Student Nonviolent Coordinating Committee (SNCC) members. James Peck, was a wealthy white Harvard graduate, another white was a minister, another a retired professor, and another a folksinger.

On May 4 in Washington, the 13 men and women divided into two teams. One boarded a Greyhound bus and the other band a Trailways bus, and both set out to penetrate the heart of white resistance to integration from the Carolinas to Mississippi.

What followed shocked the nation. When Greyhound riders arrived at Rock Hill, South Carolina, Lewis and his team were punched by angry white youths. But the police intervened, and the riders had a meal and reboarded their bus. The Trailways bus arrived two hours later to find the terminal locked.

By the time the two buses reached Alabama, white rioters armed with chains, bricks, iron pipes, and clubs were waiting for them. Outside Anniston, Alabama, a mob in cars caught up with a bus, smashed it, set it ablaze, and tried to keep the passengers inside. After they made it outside, the Freedom Riders were assaulted by a mob and were rescued by state troopers who fired into the air. The wounded were taken to a local hospital. Freedom Riders on the second bus were also beaten in Anniston. Eight members of the mob boarded the bus to slug whites in front and Blacks in the rear as the bus sped toward Birmingham.

Worse awaited in Birmingham, Alabama. FBI informant Gary Thomas Rowe, working inside the Birmingham Ku Klux Klan, told the FBI office the local police had agreed to give Klan Klavern Palace No. 13 fifteen violent minutes alone with the Freedom Riders. FBI agents informed city police officials five times of the impending attack. These reports went to the Klan, which appeared to know more about bus arrivals than the FBI.

When the first bus reached Birmingham, the eight whites who had boarded it to beat the Freedom Riders quickly left. Peck, his face and shirt covered with blood, and Charles Person led the Freedom Riders into the terminal. They looked blankly at the assembled Klansmen and reporters. When a Klansman said Person deserved to

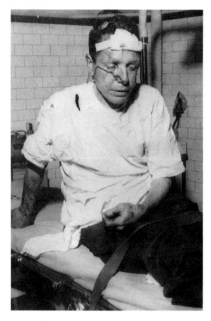

Freedom Rider James A. Peck photographed in a Birmingham hospital on May 14, 1961.

die because he injured a white man, Peck stepped forward to say it was not Person but whites who had bloodied him. This only enraged the assembled whites, including Rowe, who then began to punch Person. Peck stumbled to his defense and was again beaten. A white man, who came out of the men's room and was surprised to see rioters, was also assaulted. He was one of seven bystanders who became victim to a violence that had lost its focus and turned color-blind.

The Freedom Riders managed to escape and reach safety at the home of Reverend Fred Shuttlesworth in Birmingham. Peck was so badly beaten he had to be hospitalized. He told reporters, "I'll be back on that bus tomorrow headed for Montgomery." At 2 A.M. jittery hospital officials decided Peck's stay would endanger their hospital and discharged him. Peck used his last dime to call Reverend Shuttlesworth who picked him up in his car.

The next day photographs of the burning bus near Anniston, the attack in the Birmingham terminal, and the beaten face of James Peck reached the world media. U.S. Attorney General Robert Kennedy had been on the phone negotiating with the governor of Alabama and Reverend Shuttlesworth. Everybody agreed the battered Freedom Riders had to leave Alabama. Peck and the others said they had made their point and decided to fly to New Orleans.

Within days, more Freedom Riders boarded buses for Birmingham and were carted off to jail singing freedom songs. Most were held illegally and without charges. As President Kennedy prepared to meet Soviet Premier Nikita Khrushchev in Vienna, Austria, later in the month, the attorney general informed his brother that "the situation is getting worse in Alabama."

The President did not want to use troops and preferred to rely on "quiet diplomacy." After all, many key southern governors had been among his enthusiastic supporters in the election. Police Chief Eugene "Bull" Connor of Birmingham settled the issue when he had his deputies drag seven protesting Freedom Riders from his jail to unmarked police cars. He had them dumped with their luggage near a Tennessee railroad station and told them to take a train for Nashville and never come back.

The Freedom Riders had forced the federal government to enter the quarrel between citizens and their state governments. After a mob attacked Freedom Riders in Montgomery on May 20, Attorney General Kennedy ordered 400 federal marshals to guard the buses. The governor countered by calling out his National Guard and declaring martial law. Two days later 27 Freedom Riders were arrested in Jackson, Mississippi, and by June 12, the jails were overflowing with them.

As the civil rights crusade gained momentum, it sometimes picked up members from the enemy ranks. Robert Zellner, born and raised in Alabama, should have been in the Ku Klux Klan, for his father had been and perhaps his grandfather as well. As a college student in Mobile, young Zellner was handed a school assignment to write about race in America. He collected Ku Klux Klan booklets, White Citizens' Council leaflets, and material from the Montgomery Improvement Association. After he met with Dr. King, Reverend Abernathy, and African American students, Zellner decided he favored civil rights. The police labeled him a Communist, and friends taunted him as a "race-mixer." In 1961 he joined the SNCC just as Freedom Riders arrived in Montgomery.

A cotton worker and a civil rights worker discuss the right to vote.

> The Freedom Rides are coming through…. I'm seeing this. I'm hearing it on the radio so I go down to the city to see if I could put my body between some Klansmen and some Freedom Rider…. How could you fail to get involved?

By the fall of 1961, a number of SNCC members decided they would not return to school that term but would move into rural areas of the southern states as full-time organizers. The SNCC had made itself the movement's shock troops, and it stood ready to assist people challenging segregation, local laws, and even the Klan.

In rural Mississippi and Georgia, the SNCC besieged a power structure and a racial way of life that had held people down since the Civil War. In Albany, Georgia, students were jailed when the local African American

MISSISSIPPI
★ SUBVERSION OF ★
THE RIGHT TO VOTE

A SNCC pamphlet in 1963 describing how basic rights were being denied in Mississippi.

community mobilized peaceful prayer marches. Bernice Reagan, a SNCC organizer, recalled those days:

> We were all young people. The meetings always started with these freedom songs…. Most of the mass meeting was singing — there was more singing than there was talking.

By the end of 1961, Albany officials negotiated a settlement with SNCC leaders, but it soon became clear the officials had no intention of sticking to the agreement. They only wanted to remove their city from the nightly TV news and newspaper headlines. SNCC organizers next began an economic boycott of white businesses. The city bus company went out of business rather than desegregate. However, mass arrests of activists were resumed by Police Chief Laurie Pritchett. Since Pritchett neither used nor tolerated any violence, 1,000 demonstrators were arrested and received no national headlines. When Dr. King was arrested in Albany, President Kennedy said the city officials should negotiate in good faith with African American leaders.

Meanwhile, in such southern states as Mississippi, Alabama, and Georgia, Klansmen began to bomb churches, and some men tried to assassinate civil rights workers. Black Georgia ministers deplored "the Nazi-like reign of terror in southwest Georgia," but the bombings continued.

SNCC executive secretary James Forman called on President Kennedy to "convene a special White House Conference to discuss means of stopping the wave of terror sweeping through the South, especially where the SNCC is working on voter registration." Two days later Kennedy spoke out for voter registration drives in the South and denounced church bombings.

In 1962 the civil rights crusade also took a dramatic new turn when it started to affect the North. In New York City, African Americans and Puerto Ricans accused the Board of Education of using racial quotas in its schools. University of Chicago students protested 100 segregated apartment houses run by the college. In Englewood, New Jersey, seven Blacks and four whites sat in at City Hall to protest school segregation. Black mothers in Chicago also staged a sit-in at an elementary school to protest segregation. Rochester, New York, officials were sued for segregating schools. In Cairo, Illinois, pickets targeted a segregated pool, skating rink, and other public facilities.

But the big news of the year was the bloody confrontation between Mississippi and federal authorities when a black air force veteran, James Meredith, after 14 months of waiting, was admitted to the University of Mississippi. Supreme Court Justice Hugo Black had ordered Meredith's admission to the college.

Mississippi governor Ross Barnett pledged on radio and TV to stop Meredith and the integration of the university even if it meant Barnett's imprisonment for defying federal authority. Meredith had been helicoptered onto the campus for enrollment the next day and was protected by 500 U.S. marshals. But the governor's inflammatory statements led to a night of mayhem and murder. While Meredith read a paper and went to sleep, the marshals fought for their lives against 2,500 armed local whites.

James Meredith on his graduation day in 1963 with a degree in political science.

The appearance of United States troops in the early morning hours probably saved the marshals and Meredith. By daylight, the campus resembled a war zone. Two men lay dead, and many cars and buildings were damaged. That morning Meredith registered, went to classes, and found the students and faculty members largely courteous. Upward of 300 soldiers remained at the university to protect Meredith until he graduated a year later.

CHAPTER 18

THE BATTLE OF BIRMINGHAM

In 1960 Harrison Salisbury, a journalist who wrote about totalitarian dictators around the globe, visited Birmingham, Alabama, and found a totalitarian city. Whites ran the government and kept the 40 percent African American population from registering to vote or having a say on civic issues. From baseball parks and taxicabs to libraries and water fountains, segregation ruled. It was even illegal for Blacks and whites to play checkers with each other.

Salisbury saw that "neither Blacks nor whites talk freely." Mail was sometimes intercepted, and phones were believed to be tapped. He found that "spies... have become a fact of life."

Salisbury saw men standing guard 24 hours a day outside of black churches and Jewish synagogues, and for good reason. In 11 years 22 black churches and homes had been bombed, and two attempts had been made to dynamite synagogues. He concluded, "Birmingham's whites and Blacks share a community of fear."

Birmingham had a reputation for being the most segregated city in the United States. In the early 1960s the city was ruled by the committed segregationist Mayor Arthur Hanes and Police Commissioner Eugene "Bull" Connor, who had demonstrated his brutality toward African Americans on many occasions.

Dr. King knew that Birmingham eventually had to be tackled. Then, in late 1962, Hanes and Connor were voted out of office. King, Reverend David Abernathy, and Reverend Shuttlesworth planned a massive drive to desegregate Birmingham's downtown shopping center.

The new administration was scheduled to take over, but Hanes and Connor had challenged their removal in court and remained in power. The stage was set for a battle over segregation.

Fearing their phones were tapped, civil rights leaders used

code words. King became "JFK," and demonstrators became "baptismal candidates."

The campaign began when King and the leaders sent well-dressed, quiet black citizens to sit-in at segregated lunch counters. In the first week Connor arrested 150 women and men, and each one went to prison for six months. Demonstrations continued, and on Palm Sunday Connor used police dogs against the marchers.

Next the city passed a regulation against protest marches and issued injunctions to prohibit them. On Good Friday, 1963, King, Abernathy, and Shuttlesworth, who had announced they would ignore such injunctions, began a march into Birmingham. Connor was ready, and he jailed the leaders. King was placed in solitary confinement but released after Attorney General Robert Kennedy called a judge.

The marches continued, and so did the arrests. Civil rights leaders now sought direct federal intervention in Birmingham. Marchers gathered at the 16th Street Baptist Church on May 2 and, with schoolchildren singing "We Shall Overcome," walked into the shopping area. Hundreds, some of whom fell to their knees to pray at the approach of police, were arrested.

The next day marchers faced police dogs and huge streams of pressurized water. A stunned nationwide TV audience saw well-dressed, protesting African Americans struck down or swept along the sidewalks. Powerful jets of water that tore the bark off trees knocked people from their feet. Birmingham police then attacked the protesters with clubs. Infuriated at the brutality toward their children, Blacks began to throw bricks and broken bottles at police and firemen.

Before it was over, the number of jailed in Birmingham reached 3,300. Many were children under the age of 14. Then Burke Marshall, an assistant attorney general, arrived in town to negotiate a settlement.

The demonstrators, fearing escalating violence, postponed activities. When marches resumed the next Monday, hundreds were arrested, including about 400 children. Connor smiled and announced that he still had "plenty of room in the jail."

May 6, 1963: (top) Birmingham police use dogs to attack marchers. (bottom) Hundreds of children are arrested and led to police vans for marching into downtown Birmingham.

The white business community realized it was being strangled by the demonstrations. Sales fell, and outside investments in the city stopped. The president of U.S. Steel, the city's biggest corporation, asked business leaders to compromise. Similar advice came in phone calls from President Kennedy and members of his cabinet. Pressure also came from TV and radio coverage that showed an armed city at war with its black citizens over human rights.

On May 10 the business leaders agreed to desegregate Birmingham in 90 days, but Governor George Wallace and Mayor Hanes denounced the pact. White violence again exploded early the next morning. Bombs blew out seven African American owned businesses and homes and shattered store windows in black neighborhoods. The front half of the home of Dr. King's brother was destroyed, but his family escaped unhurt. Another bomb tore into the Gaston Hotel, headquarters for the civil rights campaign, leaving four people injured. Rioters gathered, but others held them off, saying, "Violence has always been the tactic of the white man!"

Rock singer Al Hibbler (right) was arrested for marching in Birmingham in support of civil rights protesters.

On May 12, President Kennedy mobilized federal troops outside Birmingham and made plans to federalize the National Guard. This move by Kennedy reflected two growing beliefs. One was that anarchy threatened in Birmingham. The other was that most white Americans had begun to understand that African Americans wanted nothing more revolutionary than an opportunity to work or to shop in downtown Birmingham and an equal chance in life.

That June, President Kennedy confronted a new foe in Alabama, Governor George Wallace. At his inauguration as governor that year, Wallace had announced, "I say segregation now, segregation tomorrow, segregation forever." Wallace also promised to "stand in the schoolhouse door" to halt the admission to the University of Alabama of two African Americans.

Wallace kept his pledge. He made a statement contemptuous of federal intervention and then was ordered to stand aside by a Justice Department representative. It was a dramatic display of state versus federal power and made Wallace a national figure and presidential contender.

That month President Kennedy addressed a nationwide radio and TV audience on equal rights. He said segregation was morally wrong and called for a new civil rights law that would open public facilities on an equal basis and protect the right to vote. As if to punctuate the urgency of his message, that night Medgar Evers, NAACP director in Mississippi, was gunned down in front of his Jackson home and died in his wife's arms.

The civil rights crisis in the South pushed many white women and men to support King and his demonstrators. Prominent clergymen of all faiths and both colors began to join protest marchers. Dr. Eugene Carson Blake of the United Presbyterian Church announced, "Some time or other, we are all going to have to stand and be on the receiving end of a fire hose." He then joined two dozen other clergymen in a protest march and was arrested. Many ordinary Americans wanted to find ways to express their belief that democracy had to be extended to people of color. That summer every major American city had demonstrations by thousands of African Americans and their white allies.

Mrs. Hamer, the Fighting Voter

In 1917 Fannie Lou Hamer was born in Mississippi, the 20th child born to a sharecropping family. "All of us worked in the fields, of course, but we never did get anything out of sharecropping." On August 30, 1962, she attended a meeting organized by SNCC workers James Forman, Jim Bevel, Bob Moses, and Reggie Robinson, when she and 18 others decided they would try to register to vote. The next day she traveled the 26 miles "to register to become a first-class citizen" and was arrested.

When she returned to the Marlow plantation in Ruleville, Mississippi, where she had worked for 18 years, the foreman told her, "Fannie Lou... We are not ready for this in Mississippi." She answered, "I didn't register for you, I tried to register for myself."

Hamer was fired the next day and ordered to leave. Shots were fired into the homes of several families she stayed with.

That June, Hamer and other women and men who participated in voter registration efforts were arrested by police and beaten in the jail. But Mrs. Hamer's labors for voter registration continued. In 1964 she was a major leader of the Mississippi Freedom Democratic Party and played a key role at the 1964 Democratic National Convention. ∎

CHAPTER 19

THE MARCH ON WASHINGTON

President Kennedy and Vice President Johnson developed political strategies they thought would win passage of a civil rights bill without losing the support of southern senators. They wished to rely on quiet diplomacy.

However, civil rights leaders such as King, Shuttlesworth, and Abernathy had other ideas. They felt only public pressure would ensure a civil rights bill, and they planned a march on the nation's capital. They felt that public officials, including the president, needed to see that millions of Americans favored a new law. March organizers also wanted to prove once and for all that African Americans were united, unafraid, and ready to fight for their rights, and that many whites were prepared to stand with them.

The man picked to direct the march was A. Philip Randolph, 75, who had proposed a similar march in 1941. The march date set was Sunday, August 28, 1963, which gave Randolph less than two months to prepare. Prominent Catholic, Protestant, and Jewish organizations supported the mobilization. President Kennedy publicly called it a wholesome expression of real grievances, but privately he said he was worried about violence and the threat to his party. Kennedy ordered 4,000 troops ready in Washington's suburbs and 15,000 paratroopers on alert in North Carolina.

Randolph's assistant Bayard Rustin was also worried about violence, by which he meant white violence toward marchers. But since he could not do anything about that, he concentrated on making the marchers stay comfortable. He prepared the mall before the Lincoln Memorial with hundreds of portable toilets, 21 drinking fountains, and 24 first-aid stations.

J. Edgar Hoover of the FBI had his agents call the Hollywood celebrities who had come to town and warned them to remain indoors since violence was expected. Marlon Brando, Charlton Heston, James Garner, Diahann Carroll, and Peter, Paul, and Mary were among the dozens of entertainers who arrived to participate. To make the largest march in American history more bearable, each speaker was limited to seven minutes, and uplifting music by Odetta, Harry Belafonte, Bob Dylan, Joan Baez, and Mahalia Jackson was carefully interspersed between speeches.

Singer Joan Baez was one of many entertainers who supported the civil rights movement and protested against the Vietnam War.

Two hours before the rally began, the crowd had reached 200,000 by police estimates, and latecomers were still pouring in by bus, train, plane, and on foot. The nation's capital had never seen so large a crowd. Randolph introduced Rosa Parks and other brave women of the civil rights movement.

Walter Reuther, a vice president of the AFL-CIO, referred to President Kennedy's recent trip to the Berlin Wall separating East and West Germany during the cold war. He said, "We cannot defend freedom in Berlin so long as we deny freedom in Birmingham!"

John Lewis, 23, a SNCC veteran of many beatings and southern jails, found that early copies of his speech had infuriated some of the other speakers. He had planned to discuss police brutality, the need for a "social revolution," and more jobs for people of color. Lewis agreed to tone down his remarks, and Dr. King helped him make some changes so the day's unity might be preserved.

But the rally is best remembered for King's largely unrehearsed speech that captured the crowd. His words were addressed to generations yet unborn and told of his hopes for America:

Front line of the 1963 March on Washington.

> I have a dream that my four little children will one day live in a nation where they will not be judged by the color of their skin but by the content of their character.

The bright, sunny day ended at the White House where the president greeted the march organizers. Everyone at the march, at the White House, and throughout the country talked hopefully about the new civil rights bill and an America free of racism and violence.

FURTHER READING

Adamic, Louis. *A Nation of Nations*. New York: Harper, 1944.

Barron, Milton, ed. *Minorities in a Changing World*. New York: Alfred A. Knopf, 1967.

Bernado, Stephanie. *The Ethnic Almanac*. New York: Dolphin, 1981.

Carson, Clayborne, et al. ed. *Eyes on the Prize Civil Rights Reader*. New York City: Viking Penguin, 1991.

Daniels, Roger. *Coming to America*. New York: HarperCollins, 1990.

Debo, Angie. *A History of the Indians of the United States*, rev. ed. Norman, OK: University of Oklahoma Press, 1984.

The Ethnic Chronology Series. Dobbs Ferry, NY: Oceana Publications, 1972-1990.

Evans, Sara M. *Born for Liberty: A History of Women in America*. New York: Macmillan, 1989.

Franklin, John Hope. *From Slavery to Freedom: A History of Negro Americans*, rev. ed. New York: Alfred A. Knopf, 1988.

The *In America* Series. Minneapolis, MN: Lerner Publications, 1971-1990.

Millstein, Beth and Bodin, Jeanne, eds. *We, the American Women: A Documentary History*. New York: Ozer Publishing,1977.

Moquin, Wayne, ed. *A Documentary History of the Mexican Americans*. New York: Praeger, 1972.

Seller, Maxine S. *To Seek America: A History of Ethnic Life in the United States*. Englewood, NJ: Ozer Publishing, 1977.

Takaki, Ronald. *Strangers from a Different Shore: A History of Asian Americans*. New York: Penguin Books, 1990.

Thernstrom, Stephan, ed. *Harvard Encyclopedia of American Ethnic Groups*. Cambridge, MA: Belknap Press, 1980.

INDEX